WALKING
ON
WATER

TO MY DEAR BROTHER PABLO AND SISTER NICOLE

I PRAY MY BOOK INSPIRES YOU, ENCOURAGES YOU, CONNECTS YOU TO GOD AND PREPARES YOU FOR ANY CHALLENGE YOU MAY FACE IN THE FUTURE. MAY GOD CONTINUE TO BLESS EVERYTHING YOU DO IN HIS NAME AND FOR HIS KINGDOM.

EXODUS 9:16

WITH LOVE AND GRATITUDE
YOUR BROTHER IN CHRIST

YUNG ♡ ✝

(909) 992-9203

WALKING

ON

WATER

FIVE INGREDIENTS FOR LIVING THROUGH
LIFE'S TOUGHEST CHALLENGES

RUBEN NARVÁEZ GARCIA

Published by Best Seller Publishing®, St. Augustine, FL
Best Seller Publishing® is a registered trademark.
Printed in the United States of America.
ISBN: 978-1-959840-46-6

All Scriptures from the Bible are from the
New Living Translation (NLT), unless otherwise noted.

For more information, please write:
Best Seller Publishing®
53 Marine Street
St. Augustine, FL 32084
or call 1 (626) 765-9750
Visit us online at: www.BestSellerPublishing.org

Table of Contents

INGREDIENT 3: BEING PATIENT IN AFFLICTION

INGREDIENT 4: BEING FAITHFUL IN PRAYER

INGREDIENT 5: FILLING OURSELVES WITH THE LOVE OF GOD

Introduction

This book is not just for cancer patients. It is for anyone who has gone through, is going through or is going to go through challenges that can cause them stress or worry and take them on a roller coaster of emotions.

I'm not sure what you're going through or may go through in the future. I have gone through a lot. I have been through a divorce and was left to be a full-time single parent with four children, aged six months, two years, six and seven years old at that time. I lost my oldest granddaughter, Ruby, who passed away at eleven years old. She was like a daughter to me. I have lost both of my parents—my father to colon cancer and my mom to post-COVID symptoms.

Along with my wife, I have raised six teenagers. If you haven't gone through raising a teenager, prepare yourself; it can be one of the most challenging times in your life.

I have lost jobs, businesses, homes, money and to top it all off, I am dealing with a terminal illness; I have stage 4 terminal cancer. I have been battling cancer for over four years. There have been many infusions, scans, several surgeries and terrifying, heart-stopping diagnoses and prognoses. I have been battered physically and emotionally with all these challenges.

When I was first diagnosed, I was told, "Get your affairs in order and prepare for your funeral," and that the time I had left was short–maybe a month if I was lucky. God has spared me. I feel God has prolonged my life for me to open my eyes to see how blessed we all really are. He has taught me so much the last four years and has worked incredible miracles in my life. I have to tell the world what God has done and will do for anyone who chooses to trust Him. With the treatment I am on, the doctors say life expectancy is five years; those five years will be up soon. The truth is, only God knows when our last day of life is. We all only have today. After everything I've gone through, I am still here–full of faith, full of hope and with a smile on my face, enjoying my life.

I have lived longer than expected, and the last four years haven't just been challenges and struggles. I have finally stopped life to spend quality time with my family. I have traveled to so many places and I have done things I never would've imagined. My vision of life has changed, all thanks to having cancer and knowing my life was coming to an end soon. I have written this book hoping to inspire you–to give you the hope, the encouragement and the help that you will need to get through any challenge. Enjoy reading as you enter into the last four years of my life's challenges, stories and struggles.

Philippians 4:12-13 says, "I know how to live on almost nothing or with everything. I HAVE LEARNED THE SECRET OF LIVING IN EVERY SITUATION, whether it is with a full stomach or empty, with plenty or little. For I can do everything through Christ, who gives me strength."

My friend Marco Chavez asked me one day, "You're going through the challenge of fighting cancer, your granddaughter just passed away and now your mom has passed away. I speak to you, and it seems like nothing is going on, like everything is okay. How do you do it?" He asked me to share the recipe.

I told him the recipe, and now I am sharing with you how I am able to cope with such things, maintain my calm and be at peace. I shared a couple of these Scriptures with him: the recipe, the secret of living through every situation.

In my book, there are 5 ingredients:

1. Fear of God

2. Being Joyful in Hope

3. Being Patient in Affliction

4. Being Faithful in Prayer

5. Filling Ourselves with the Love of God

Applying these 5 ingredients to your life will open doors to happiness and give you the freedom you desire and the peace that no money can buy.

In every situation, there's a lesson to be learned. Having cancer, I've learned to depend completely on God, 100 percent. I knew right away I wasn't going to be able to handle the stress, worry or uncertainty of this problem, so I gave it all to Him. I've learned that sometimes we have to go through difficulty to open our eyes to see how blessed we really are. We need to appreciate everything God gives us.

WHY THE TITLE *WALKING ON WATER?*

The story of Jesus walking on water in Matthew 14 has always thrilled me. All of the stories of the miracles Jesus did make me wish I was there. I would've loved to have witnessed at least one of His miracles in real life. Well, God has granted me the gift of not only witnessing a miracle but living it. I was in death's clutches; there was no hope or future. Cancer had come in, and I was drowning in it. But God, through my faith in Him, changed everything. He reached down and grabbed me, just like Jesus did to Peter, and pulled me up out of the problem I was drowning in.

He has allowed me to walk on water. I am living the miracle. Every day that I wake up is a miracle; I am walking on water everywhere I go. My life is exciting! It has its challenges, but I am loving the new life and opportunity God has given me. I am no longer afraid of anything. He has given me the courage to take down Goliath; He has resurrected me. Even when I am in total darkness my faith still shines. My perspective on life has done a *one-eighty*; I am really living now, living by faith, walking on water.

> [25]About three o'clock in the morning Jesus came toward them, walking on the water. [26]When the disciples saw him walking on the water, they were terrified. In their fear, they cried out, "It's a ghost!" [27]But Jesus spoke to them at once. "Don't be afraid," he said. "Take courage. I am here!" [28]Then Peter called to him, "Lord, if it's really you, tell me to come to you, walking on the water." [29]"Yes, come," Jesus said. So Peter went over the side of the boat and walked on the water toward Jesus. [30]But when he saw the strong wind and the waves, he was terrified and began to sink. "Save me, Lord!" he shouted. [31]Jesus immediately reached out and grabbed him. "You have so little faith," Jesus said. "Why did you doubt me?" [32]When they climbed back into the boat, the wind stopped. [33]Then the disciples worshiped him. "You really are the Son of God!" they exclaimed. –Matthew 14:25-33 NLT

> Ruben Narváez Garcia

FEAR OF GOD

PROVERBS 1:7

The fear of the Lord is the beginning of knowledge,
but fools despise wisdom and instruction.

Chapter One

IN THE BEGINNING

Narváez family, 2002.

PSALMS 115:11
All you who fear the Lord, trust the Lord!
He is your helper and your shield.

I was born December 1,1965 to Mexican parents. My dad was born in Nuevo León, Monterrey, Mexico, and my mom was born in Matamoros, Tamaulipas, Mexico. My parents met through my family. My mom's older brother is married to my dad's older sister. They began dating and were later married. We lived in the Maravilla projects in East Los Angeles when I was born and moved around to a few places in East LA.

The house we lived in the longest was on Brannick Avenue. My grandmother (Mom's mom) lived next door along with a few of my uncles on the same block. My dad's family lived nearby on Kern Avenue, and eventually my dad's side of the family all moved to La Puente, California. My mom was sixteen when they got married, my dad twenty-three. I was born when my mom was seventeen, and by that time my dad was about to turn twenty-five.

I was raised throughout my childhood in a very tight-knit, close family. We did everyone's parties together, spent weekends together and went on family vacations together with both sides of the family. We drove several times by caravan to Monterrey, Mexico, to visit family. After me, my brother Edward was born in 1968 and then my sister Rachel was born in 1971.

Around a year later, my parents separated and then divorced when I was about eight years old. It was a difficult time seeing my parents go through all of that. My life was shattered, not only from my parents ending their relationship but also from the domestic violence I witnessed. It was emotionally heartbreaking watching their marriage unravel. My mom remarried and had five children with my stepdad. My dad remarried and had two children with my stepmom, so I am the oldest of ten siblings. I was raised with my mom and my seven siblings until I was eighteen, and at that time I moved out.

I was already working, so I got my own place and I got together with my kids' mom; she was sixteen years old at the time and we soon started our family. My son Ruben Jr. was born in September of 1985, and eleven months later in August 1986 we welcomed my daughter Melissa. In October 1990 came my son Andres (Andy), and in June 1992 came my son Christopher. About six months after Christopher was born, my wife and I separated. I kept my four kids; eventually I got sole custody and raised them by myself. It was the biggest challenge I had ever faced in my life.

Here I was, twenty-seven years old, with four kids (two still in diapers), and I didn't know how to wash or cook. Being my prideful self, I thought, *Piece of cake; I can handle it*. I got a babysitter and kept going to work for the next couple of weeks. Before I knew it, the clothes hamper was full and the kids were tired of eating TV dinners. I decided to quit my job, go on welfare and take on the job of Mr. Mom.

I would call my mom and my grandmother daily to ask how to cook certain dishes and how to wash our clothes. Back then there was no social media or YouTube; the only technology we had was pagers, and I did not own a computer. It took me eight months to learn how to maintain my home. After those eight months of being home with my kids, I became an expert in cooking, cleaning and washing, and of course taking care of my kids. I was now officially a homemaker, but it was time to get back to work because welfare was not enough to live on. I went back to work and continued my routine of being a homemaker too.

In October of 1995 I visited my church for the first time. On November 5, 1995, I made the commitment to follow Jesus and was baptized as a disciple of His. For the next six months I tried to restore my marriage but it didn't work out, so we separated again. As my ex began another relationship in July of 1996, I moved forward with a dissolution of marriage. On January 27, 1997, I was divorced and also continued to have sole custody of my four kids. During the time I was going through my divorce, I met my current wife, Rosalba, in the singles ministry at our church. We got to know each other pretty well. I learned she was from Mexico City, that she also came from a family of ten siblings and that she had come to the United States in 1994. She was very caring and spiritually sound, and my kids and I grew fond of her.

By the time my divorce went through, I knew Rosalba was the woman I wanted to spend the rest of my life with, so we were married on February 15, 1997. She is a truly amazing woman. Here she was, twenty-five years old, never been married and no children, and all of a sudden she has a husband and four kids. What a challenge! A month after we were married, she became pregnant with our son Gabriel, who was born on December 11, 1997. Five years later, our daughter Gaby was born in September 2002.

We took our first trip to Mexico City in December 2004. We all packed up: my wife, four kids, my dad, his wife and my nephew, and we drove down in our van for thirty-six hours. I highly recommend driving, as you can stop in all the towns and explore every place you pass through. I was amazed with all of the places we visited. I was in love not only with my wife but also with this country that I was beginning to explore. We spent time with her family and came back home after two weeks out there.

As our kids grew up, they moved on and started their own lives. Grandchildren became a part of our lives. First came Ruby, then Audrina, Briella, Jaslene and a few years later, Alaia and Marley. Currently two of our children still live at home—Gabriel and Gaby, our youngest.

From early 2017 through the summer, I lost around forty-five pounds. My wife and kids kept saying something was wrong with me. They saw I kept getting slimmer and slimmer through those months. I also had bloody stools for about six of those months.

At their request, I went to the doctor to have bloodwork done, and to see why I had lost so much weight and find out about the bloody stools. All of my tests came back fine; nothing to worry about, the doctor said. I had a probe done and the doctor said it was hemorrhoids. He prescribed some suppositories and the bloody stools stopped. He recommended a colonoscopy to confirm that nothing else was going on because my father had passed away from colon cancer a few years earlier.

We had a family meeting to go over the results, and at that point my family members asked me to have the colonoscopy to make sure nothing was wrong. They all chipped in to pay for it since I didn't have medical insurance, so I went ahead and did the procedure. Those results came back, and the doctor said my colon looked good—that it was clean—no polyps or anything else that might cause worry. After that I was convinced that I was fine. I said to my family, "You see, I'm fine."

Well, I feel like God said, "I'm going to cause something to happen so they'll find out what's really wrong with you." In late November I got what's called "frozen shoulder" on both of my shoulders.

It's a rare illness. Doctors aren't sure what causes it. It's extremely painful and debilitating. Doctors see it in some patients with diabetes; I don't have diabetes. Usually one shoulder gets frozen, but in my case, both shoulders were frozen. The arm locks into the shoulder capsule, and after that you're completely unable to move your arms. It's EXTREMELY painful; I didn't sleep well for three months.

I wasn't sure what was going on, and I told people what was happening to me (big mistake, I should've gone to see a doctor) and of course everyone thought they knew what to do or they had a solution. I made many bad decisions seeking treatment from *sobadores*, people trying to unlock my shoulders by pulling them apart, and all types of creams and lotions; nothing worked. Lesson learned: go see a doctor when you're sick. Your friends, parents, neighbors and so on aren't doctors, so stop asking for their opinions. Doctors are specially trained and will recommend the medicine or treatment necessary for you to become well.

On December 28, 2017, I drove down to Ensenada, Mexico, by referral from one of my son's friends (thank you, Saiko!) to see a radiologist. I had to go down to Mexico since I still didn't have medical insurance. My wife and I, along with our daughter Gaby, my nephew Alex and niece Yvonne, stopped in Tijuana. This was my nephew and niece's first time in Mexico. At the airport there we picked up my mother-in-law, who had flown in from Mexico City.

From there, we drove down to Ensenada to see the radiologist. I asked to have MRIs done on both of my shoulders, and while I was there, I asked the price for a CT scan of my abdomen and chest. "Three hundred dollars," the lady said. "Let's do it," I replied. I finished up my MRIs and CT scan, and the doctor said to come back the next day to pick up the report.

We left and went to eat some fresh seafood at the Mercado Negro at the port of Ensenada. After eating, we went to La Bufadora and spent the afternoon there enjoying "the blowhole" and buying souvenirs. We drove back to downtown Ensenada and had some tacos. My niece and nephew said they were the best tacos they'd ever tasted. We walked the streets of downtown, sightseeing, buying more souvenirs and walking by some of the bars and nightclubs Ensenada is famous for. We headed back to our hotel after our walk, and the next morning we got ready and went to breakfast, then off to pick up the report.

We went into the office, and before the nurse handed us the report she noticed a note that said, "Tell patient not to leave, I'd like to speak to him." So the nurse walked us into the doctor's office.

At that point my wife said, "Something must be wrong." She was feeling nervous about the meeting. The doctor and his father (also a radiologist) came in. They sat down and he said, "I'm really glad you did the CT scan. What we found is that you have stage 4 cancer. You have a massive tumor on your left kidney, and it has metastasized to both of your lungs."

"What about my shoulders?" I asked.

He said, "Forget about your shoulders. This is a matter of life and death. You need to see an oncologist right away."

As we walked out of the office into the lobby, I paused and realized what the doctor had said. I remembered my dad had had stage 4 cancer and died. I realized at that moment what the news meant. I broke down and began to cry uncontrollably.

FINAL THOUGHT

My mind was going one hundred miles per hour. I thought, *I'm gonna die!* Looking at my wife, I couldn't imagine her as a widow; I couldn't leave her alone. I thought about the pain it was going to cause her. My kids were still young. I looked at Gaby playing outside through the office door, knowing she still needed me. All my kids needed me, and what about my granddaughters?

The news was going to cause my mom so much pain; she was going to constantly worry. My whole family was on my mind. *I won't be able to walk my daughter down the aisle when she gets married someday. I'm going to miss out on so many events, It's over! How can this be?* I was so unprepared for the news. *I came for my shoulders and now I find out life is over! I have plans. There's so much left to do. Life is so unfair!!! I have just lost control of my life ...*

Chapter Two

SUDDEN TURNS

Gaby dressed up for her party.
Narváez family at the party February 3, 2018.

As the doctor read the results, my wife later said she felt time
had stopped; everything turned gray. She was in total shock, not
knowing how to respond. It felt like she was dreaming; it was
the worst news she had ever heard. She said I turned pale as
the doctor gave us the news. My wife had always felt something

was not right with my health. She knew in her heart that I was gravely ill, but hearing the doctor confirm it was heartbreaking. Her mom had become a widow at a young age and was left to raise ten kids on her own.

There in the lobby, my wife consoled me for a bit, and then I gathered myself. My family was outside, and I didn't want them to see me upset. I didn't want to break the news to them yet.

As we drove home, I sent a message to my kids and to my siblings about the results.

As you can imagine, everyone responded to my message right away. Everyone was as shocked as we were, and all were sending comforting messages. "We'll get through this, Dad!" "Don't worry, bro, you can beat this!" The trip home was a total blur.

During this time, we had been planning my daughter Gaby's quinceañera, which was scheduled for February 3. We met with my family and discussed what to do next. I told them that I felt fine, that we should wait until after the party to go into the hospital, that everything was already scheduled and paid for and that I wasn't sure what would happen once I went into the hospital. *Would they start chemo right away? Surgery? Would I make it to February? Would I be mobile?*

I decided to wait. A couple of months had gone by and the pain in my shoulders continued. I had minimal movement in my arms. I still needed help getting dressed and was feeling anxious and desperate, both at not having mobility in my arms and also from the pain it was causing. I felt like I had become a burden on my family. I was frustrated at not being able to work and also was wondering about the cancer I was diagnosed with. Life as I knew it had changed completely. I couldn't help around the house; I felt like I couldn't do anything!

Not being able to use my arms was eye-opening. You never realize how much you need something until you are unable to use it. I couldn't drive and I couldn't cook for myself, which are things we take for granted. February couldn't come fast enough. We continued with the preparations; there was still so much to do. I needed to get my tuxedo, my wife's dress and all of the stuff for the candy table, and I had to prepare the slideshow and rehearse the presentation for her entrance—whew, lots to do. Planning the event helped keep my mind off my cancer diagnosis, but it still lingered in my head. I wrestled with it but continued to pray and not let it get the best of me. I had a big celebration coming up and I was excited for that. The day finally arrived. The doubt and worry were gone; I had made it! I thanked God for allowing me the privilege to be alive and to attend my daughter's celebration. I was so grateful that I was going to be able to enjoy and live out this big event. By this time, I was definitely feeling more fatigued, so I prayed to God to give me the strength to get through this long-awaited day.

That morning we were all up early and ready for the videographer and photographer's arrival. It started with pictures and video of my daughter getting ready and pictures of her room and her wardrobe. We also had pictures and videos with my daughter and did interviews of the family giving her well-wishes. The limousine arrived to pick up my daughter and her friends so they could go for a ride before meeting up at the hall to take group pictures.

We walked into the hall and waited inside while everyone began to arrive. My wife, my daughters and my sons stood at the entrance, welcoming the guests. All of our family and friends began to arrive—uncles and aunts, cousins and friends—everyone with big smiles on their faces, everyone excited for the celebration. Greeting everyone brought me so much joy and at the same time sadness. Would this be my last party? Would this be the last time I saw all of these people? As people greeted me, they wished me well. Some said, "We're praying for you," others thanked me for my friendship and others told me how much they loved me. There were smiles along with tears as we hugged. The hall filled up with guests and the party began.

The music started and all the guests stood up to receive my daughter and her court. My beautiful granddaughters in their lovely princess dresses walked in, preparing the way for my daughter's grand entrance. The introduction rang through the building: "Presenting Gabriela Narváez!" As everyone applauded, my daughter walked in like a peacock, full of pride and her head held high, the center of attention.

Next we had her service, given by our pastor Carlos "Joel" Serna. He gave us a great message of what turning fifteen meant for our culture and for Gaby as well. He reminded us of each one of our roles and our responsibility as a village to continue to raise our children in the path of God. During the service, my wife and I presented Gaby with a promise ring. I said to Gaby, "I don't like to make promises because promises are usually broken. With this ring, I don't make a promise; I make the commitment to love you and protect you in and under all circumstances, to be by you and support you for the rest of my life. I will be the hand reaching out to lift you up, always. May it serve as a reminder of my love for you."

The service ended in a prayer followed by the presentation we had rehearsed for. It had been challenging because I didn't have much movement in my arms. The idea was to transmit a silhouetted image of my daughter as a baby and the steps of her growing into a fifteen-year-old girl. We all can relate that our children grow up so quickly, so we chose the song "No Crezcas Mas" (which means "don't grow anymore") to play in the background, with a sheer white curtain hanging and a spot-light behind it. Try to imagine the images. I walked behind the curtain, reached out and picked up my niece Valentina, who was a few months old, and held her up and then put her down. Next, I walked my granddaughter Briella into the scene. You could see the image of me and her in her fancy dress, and she reached out her hands and held mine.

We danced a few steps, swaying side to side, and then I twirled her. As she twirled, she danced out of the scene. Next, in came Audrina, who was a little older and did the same routine, and next came Ruby and did the same. Every girl who walked in was bigger and older. After Ruby, Gaby walked into the scene with her fancy dress, and I heard everyone scream and applaud. Gaby did the same scene, and we ended it with me kissing her forehead. We walked out from behind the curtain, and I saw many people crying, especially the women. The applause continued for a good while.

We walked out to the crowd and received many hugs. People were telling us what a beautiful presentation it was, and how it reminded them of their children and how fast they grow up. It was an emotional moment that set the tone for the rest of the evening; everyone's hearts were overflowing with emotion. Right after, we had a presentation of gifts. My daughter Melissa was wearing her crown, which was bigger than Gaby's (being she was the older sister). She removed Gaby's crown, then removed her crown and placed it on Gaby's head, signifying the new princess of the family. Then Gaby sat down, and Melissa, together with her husband, my son-in-law Hector, removed Gaby's shoes and placed heels on her feet, signifying a step into womanhood.

Now, with her new heels on, we did the father-daughter dance and then she danced her waltz. We went to a delicious dinner made by my friends the Barrazas, while music played in the background. After we dined, we continued the party with the dance; everyone was enjoying the event. We had a picture booth set up and the photographer was taking pictures of all the guests with Gaby. During the celebration many guests spoke to me personally to ask how I was feeling and if there was any news on my condition. I let them know I would be going into the hospital in a few days to see what the future held.

While I spoke to people, my emotions would overwhelm me; there was a lot of uncertainty of what was to come, but my response was "Only God knows," and "I will trust whatever happens is His will." Some of the conversations were almost as if we were saying goodbye. I was concentrating on enjoying the day and not focusing too much on my illness; for now I was celebrating my daughter's party and that day of life God had given me. I was feeling so blessed, and the joy I felt was incredible. What a party! We said goodbye to all of our guests and waited at the hall for the rented equipment to be picked up and the DJ to take all of his stuff. My wife and I stood there until the end. We looked at each other and said, "We did it," as we smiled and hugged. We went home and rested from a long day and the many months of planning.

FINAL THOUGHT

I am glad I was able to enjoy my daughter's quinceañera. It was a blast. A few months ago, I thought that I may not make it this far. But I did, thank God! I'm not sure what comes next, but I will make the best of every day; each day will be a celebration of life. I may not be able to move my arms much, but I am still alive. I pray that I will always remember to treasure each moment and not take for granted all of the blessings God has given me.

Chapter Three

AN ANGEL IN
COWBOY BOOTS

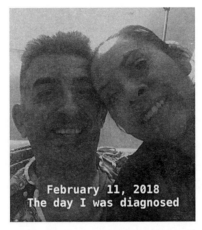

February 11, 2018, shortly after being diagnosed and
given the prognosis of having a short time to live.

PROVERBS 3:5-8

*Trust in the Lord with all your heart; do not depend
on your own understanding. Seek his will in all you
do, and he will show you which path to take. Don't
be impressed with your own wisdom. Instead, fear
the Lord and turn away from evil. Then you will have
healing for your body and strength for your bones.*

February 7, 2018. My mom and I drove to the hospital with my radiology results from Ensenada in hand. We walked into the emergency room, and I checked in.

A doctor called me in, and when we sat down, I explained that the radiologist had told me that I had stage 4 cancer and handed over the images and report. She asked if I had medical insurance, and at this point I still didn't. She had me go to a window and apply for emergency medical aid. I filled out the application and was denied; the lady said I didn't qualify. I went back and let the doctor know that I didn't qualify, so she had me take a seat and wait while she made some phone calls.

I sat there and listened to her call around to several hospitals and heard her explain my situation over and over. They all asked if I had insurance, and of course the response was no, so they all said they couldn't take me without insurance.

She grabbed the paperwork and images I gave her and said, "Sorry, we can't help you; I called other hospitals and they can't take you without insurance either." She said to get insurance and then come back.

It was a really emotional moment, because when they were sending me away, I was already thinking, *I'm dead.*

As I walked away, the head doctor of the emergency room (I call him an angel in cowboy boots) asked the woman doctor where I was going.

She said, "He doesn't have insurance. I called several hospitals, and they won't take him without insurance anywhere."

He told her, "You can't send him away; he's got stage 4 cancer." The (angel) head doctor called me back. "Sir," he said, "listen, don't worry about the insurance. We have people who donate money to the hospital specifically for people like you without insurance; we're going to take care of you." He then told the other doctor, "Take him inside, get him admitted and let's start running tests." And then the angel in cowboy boots traveled onward to his next assignment, for further lives to save.

The woman doctor took me inside. They got me into a room and the testing began. MRIs, CT scans with contrast, bloodwork, urinalysis, biopsy of my lung—they performed so many tests. At this point I still thought there was a possibility that it wasn't cancer. I thought maybe it was just a big cyst that had grown and that it would show up through the biopsy.

After being in the hospital for three days, having numerous tests and exams done, four doctors walked into my room: the head doctor of the hospital, an oncologist, a radiologist and a urologist. The room was filled with my family: my wife, my kids, my siblings and my nephews and nieces. The oncologist asked, "How are you feeling?"

"I'm feeling pretty good," I said.

"Sir, we have gone over your tests and are here to give you your results. The CT scans with contrast, MRIs and biopsy results show you have stage 4 terminal cancer."

"What does 'terminal' mean?" I asked.

"Terminal means just that—it means you are going to die. You have a massive tumor on your left kidney that has metastasized to both of your lungs, to your inferior vena cava (IVC) and to your heart. The vena cava is plugged with cancer, and in your heart it has spread to the whole right side, into both chambers."

"How much time do I have left?" I asked.

"It could be a day, a week or a month if you're lucky. It would be irresponsible of me to give you a date, but it won't be long; you have a lot of cancer. My advice is, get your affairs in order and make preparations for your funeral. Although I will tell you this, scientifically we don't have an explanation of what's going on with you. With the amount of cancer you have, you should be bedridden 24/7, under constant care and in extreme pain, but you have none of that."

Upon hearing that, I thought of what he had said first: "Prepare for your funeral." Thinking back to that moment, I remember so many thoughts running through my mind: *I'm about to leave my family; my wife and kids still need me; I'm not going to be able to see my kids get married; I won't be around for my granddaughters' quinceañeras; I'm going to die!* I thought of the pain it was going to cause my family, which was one of the most heartbreaking thoughts.

As I calmed down a bit I thought, *Okay, if I'm not in a condition that I'm supposed to be, that scientifically they can't explain why I'm not bedridden, in extreme pain and so on, then God's got me; He's already working. God has a plan!* I was trying so hard to stay hopeful and positive.

My family and I were all shocked by the news. We all discussed the results and tried to make sense of it. I know I was thinking about my dad's passing from colon cancer. I didn't want it to end the same way. It was a humbling moment. Then everyone stepped out of the room to give my wife and me some time alone. I don't think we have ever hugged each other so tight, and as sadness overcame us, we had a good cry and then prayed.

I was then discharged that day with no options; I was basically sent home to die.

FINAL THOUGHT

This was a hopeless and hopeful moment for me. I was feeling so many different emotions. I was confused, scared, lost in my thoughts. I am not afraid of dying, but there was a deep sorrow in my heart. I thought of the pain my death would cause my wife, my children, my siblings and my friends. I reached for any comfort I could think of, and that comfort was God. With God there is always hope and with all of the news I received, there was still hope that God would perform a miracle. I am so grateful for my relationship with Him.

Chapter Four

SECOND OPINION

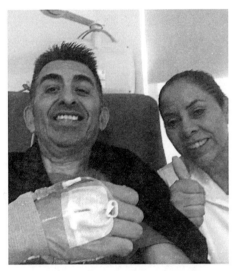

Second infusion March 29, 2018.

P R O V E R B S   1 9 : 2 3
*Fear of the Lord leads to life, bringing
security and protection from harm.*

A few days later, the urologist who had come into the room with the other doctors called me and said he wanted to see me. I told him I didn't have insurance, but he said, "It's okay, I'll see you for free."

I went in for my appointment along with my daughter Melissa and my sister Ana to see the urologist. He said he was really worried for me, that I had a lot of cancer, and I was at a high risk of a pulmonary embolism and other problems. He suggested I try a chemo pill called Sutent. "At least try something," he said. He reaffirmed that my condition was very serious—how close I was to death—and wished me the best. I really appreciated him seeing me for free. I felt like he really cared; God bless that man.

When I got outside of the building, I began to cry. "That's not the news I wanted to hear," I said. I was hoping he was going to give me good news, but it was just a reminder that I was going to die.

My sister Ana said she was going to look into getting insurance for me and getting a second opinion at another hospital. She called City of Hope Cancer Hospital, and they told her they would give me an appointment only if I had insurance. I was finally able to get medical insurance, so she called late February to get me an appointment. The person on the phone told her someone had just canceled an appointment for March 1 and if we liked, we could schedule it.

"Yes! We'll take it," my sister said. My new insurance was going to be effective on March 1, so it worked out perfectly. Amazing how it all worked out.

The day came, and I went in for my appointment, accompanied by my wife and my sister. The doctor already had all of my test results and images, so she was well informed. She looked into what they could offer as treatment, scrolling through lists of possibilities.

"There's a clinical trial I might be able to get you on but because the cancer is in your vena cava, it will more than likely disqualify you. It's a combination of two medicines that you can do through an infusion. We normally install a port, but because you have so much cancer in the vena cava, heart and lungs, it will be too dangerous; it can cause you to have a stroke or a pulmonary embolism. It's too risky. Let me send in the request and see what they say," she said.

The doctor submitted the request, and while we were there, it was approved. "Great," she said, "they approved it. We can try this treatment and see if it helps. I can't guarantee anything but it's worth a try. So far, in one out of four patients, we've seen some favorable results. The goal is to try and shrink the cancer enough so we can do a debulking surgery and remove the majority of the cancer. We can't do anything with the lungs, but we can try to get the rest out if we can shrink it. I can schedule you in for March 8 for your first infusion. Would you like to try this treatment?"

"Let's do it," I said. "I have nothing to lose; my only other choice is to wait and die."

I went in for my first infusion appointment accompanied by my son Gabriel and my daughter Melissa. I was received with excellent service and did my infusion of both medicines. While waiting, we put together a puzzle and played some games until my infusion was done. We went home, and I rested.

I continued the infusions every three weeks, and as time passed, I began to have some side effects. One of the first side effects was a really bad dry mouth. I asked the doctor about it, and she said the medicine had burned my saliva glands and that it was permanent damage. She suggested sipping water and mints or hard candies to keep my mouth moist. I got hand-foot syndrome, folliculitis, mouth sores and other side effects related to the medicine.

This was just the beginning of my journey. Little did I know that this was just a glimpse of what was to come.

FINAL THOUGHT

I'm not sure if this medicine is going to help but glad at least I'm on some kind of treatment. I am not afraid to die; I know where I am going—Heaven is an amazing place. Not that I already want to leave but I'm at peace with it. There is a deep sorrow in my heart when I consider my death. What pains me is when I die, I think of the pain my wife, my kids, siblings, family and friends are going to go through. Death of a loved one can be unbearable. May God comfort them.

Chapter Five

FATHERS AND SONS

Ruben (middle) and my sons (left to right: Ruben
Jr., Gabriel, Chris, and Andy) at the largest
pyramid in the world at Cholula, Puebla.

PSALMS 127:3-5
Children are a gift from the Lord;
they are a reward from him. Children born to a
young man are like arrows in a warrior's hands.
How joyful is the man whose quiver is full of them!

After being diagnosed in February of 2018 and receiving the news from the doctor that I had a short time to live, I thought, *There are a lot of things I still want to do*. One of those things was to travel. There were many places I wanted to visit and see in Mexico, so I planned a trip out there. I wanted to spend time with my family, so the first trip I went on was with my four sons. I told them, "I'm not sure how long I have left, but I would like to take a guys' trip to Mexico so we could spend some time together." They all agreed and made arrangements with their jobs to take some time off work.

I wanted to spend time with my sons so I could take some time to talk to all of them and express some feelings I had. As they were growing up, I was very strict with them, especially with my two oldest children. The other four I was strict with too; I had a little more patience, but I still felt I'd hurt them. I wanted to sincerely apologize for any hurt I had caused them from disciplining them and scolding them when they were younger. As they grew up, I lacked patience and respect toward my kids. When they asked me for permission to go out, my answer was usually no. I was afraid of leaving them unprotected; that if I wasn't around, they might be misled, or so many other things could go wrong. I don't know if everyone feels like I do, but I've always wished my kids could be young again and give me a chance to do it all over again. I didn't have a plan as to when I would talk to the boys, but I figured we would be driving many hours so there would be plenty of time to talk while we were driving.

The day came for us to fly out. Andy and I flew out together. Chris caught up to us the next day, and Ruben Jr. and Gabriel came a day after that.

The first day Andy and I went to see a pyramid and some ruins in Malinalco, which is about three hours from Mexico City. We arrived and walked around town, where we checked out the church and a few shops. We then walked into the archeological site to see the pyramid and ruins. We walked up more than 420 steps to get to the site. What an amazing place! We walked through the whole place and enjoyed this historical sacred Aztec Empire site where the elite Jaguar and Eagle warriors did their training.

After that, we drove to Toluca to see the Cosmovitral, a botanical garden and stained-glass museum. What an amazing place. The stained glass surrounding the upper walls of the whole building are incredible. The colors, shapes and images on the stained glass are nothing short of spectacular! All the flowers, plants, shrubs and trees are from different regions in Mexico. There is a Japanese garden—an area with many succulents and flowers that almost look fake, the colors and shapes are so beautiful.

We picked up Chris at the airport the next morning and from there went to La Casa Azul, the home where Frida Kahlo was raised and lived as a young girl. It's a beautiful bright blue throughout the property, hence the name La Casa Azul, or blue house. There is so much history in that place, including many of Frida's paintings, drawings, photographs and other art throughout the whole house.

We left there and went straight to the Aztec pyramids in Teotihuacan. When you walk into the place, you are immediately amazed at the sight of the humongous sun pyramid. It reminded me of the first time I saw the Grand Canyon—this place definitely has that wow factor. You walk in toward the pyramid and climb the many steep stairs to arrive at the top. Standing at the top, you are overtaken by the energy of the place and left in awe as you view the valley from the top of the sun pyramid. You are also able to see several structures below and imagine what the city looked like when the Aztecs lived there. For me, it is the climax of all pyramids in Mexico.

After that, we left, and Andy and Chris went back to the hotel. Later that night, I went to pick up Ruben Jr. and Gabriel at the airport. We stopped to eat some tacos then headed back to the hotel. The next day, we headed out to Puebla to see the Fuerte de Guadalupe, the place where the Mexican army defeated Napoleon and his French army on Cinco de Mayo. We went through the museum and as the staff explained all of the history and showed us all of the historical items, we were all intrigued at what an incredible place we were standing in.

As we were walking through, Ruben Jr. and Gabriel met the director of the museum, Miguel Diaz, outside on the patio. He introduced himself and asked where they were from. They told him the reason for our trip, and he asked to meet me. As I walked out with Andy and Chris, they introduced us, and we shook hands and embraced. We talked for a while, sharing stories, and here began a great friendship. He offered us a tour through the rooftop of the fort to take some pictures with a view of the whole valley below. Again, what an amazing experience!

I have gone back to the forts with my wife and met up with Miguel. To this day, we're in contact and encourage one another often. You never know who you will meet along your travels and who your next new friend will be.

On our drive to Cholula, I felt the nudge to pour my heart out to my boys. Although I know my sons love me and I am convinced they know how much I love them, I told them that part of taking this trip was that I wanted to take a moment and apologize for my bad attitude toward them many times throughout the years. I asked them to forgive me and said that it was something that had bothered me for a long time. My eyes filled with tears and my voice was shaky as I continued to talk.

They stopped me, and Ruben Jr. said, "No, Dad, you don't have to apologize; you're a great father."

Andy added, "Look at how we turned out; I would say we turned out pretty good thanks to you."

"If anything, we owe you an apology for our rebelliousness," Chris said. "I'm sorry, Dad, for all the pain I caused you. I rebelled at an early age and made life really hard for you."

It was awesome to hear their comments. I had had so much guilt for so long, and now I finally felt some relief. We kept talking about some of the things we all went through and laughed it off. I love my sons; what great forgiving hearts they have.

We arrived at Cholula to see the largest pyramid in the world. We walked through the tunnels and got to the outskirts of the pyramid. Most of the pyramid is buried underground but there's plenty of it above ground too. It's a site you have to visit to see the greatness and feel the history of this place.

We ate and left for Mexico City to catch the Cruz Azul soccer game at Estadio Azteca. We arrived late and by the time we found parking, the game was over.

We went to dinner with my cousin Rafa Baca after his game. We stayed over at his house and left the next morning to go to the Castillo de Chapultepec, a castle that President Porfirio Diaz lived in and decorated with a lot of European furniture. There are marble floors imported from Italy and France along with incredible art throughout the castle. Outside the castle are great views of Mexico City, making for some awesome pictures.

We left there and dropped Chris off at the airport so he could fly back, as he only had a few days off work. The next day, we went to Queretaro. On the way there, we stopped to eat some delicious barbacoa for breakfast. After our meal, we arrived in Queretaro, did some sightseeing, ate again and did a tour of the church, Templo y Convento de La Santa Cruz de Los Milagros. In the garden grows a thorn bush whose thorns are in the shape of a cross. It's the only place in the world with this special thorn bush. It is said that one day a friar was in the garden, and while praying, stuck his staff into the ground, and eventually the thorn bush grew with thorns shaped like a cross.

The thorns come in many sizes, but they are all shaped like a cross. It's a pretty cool thing to see.

Next, we were off to San Miguel de Allende. It's a beautiful old colonial town with cobblestoned streets and picturesque buildings. We walked through a few streets, then through the main plaza to view the Gothic church at the center, the Parroquia de San Miguel Arcangel. We then went from San Miguel to Tula, Hidalgo. There we went to see an incredible pyramid built by the Toltecs. Standing at the top of the pyramid with the almost fifteen-foot-tall atlantes statues is an amazing experience. The surrounding ruins are amazing there too.

We bought some souvenirs and took off to the Grutas de Tolantongo. We wanted to end our trip there because it's an amazing place and it would be somewhere we could just relax after our trip. This is the ultimate place for a relaxing retreat.

We left later that day and headed back to the airport to come home. I had a great time hanging out with my boys, exploring Mexico and its rich culture and history, not to mention the delicious food, of course.

While on vacation, on one of the nights I went to visit my church. I arrived and found my good friend Marco Chavez, the pastor from the church in the Iztacalco area. He had invited me to share my testimony with his congregation. At the start of the service he introduced me, and I came onstage to share my testimony with the congregation and give them a message about all the wonderful things God is doing in my life.

I started off telling them that I had gone through many things in my life: a divorce, lost jobs and many other situations that had caused me worry, stress and anger. I hadn't gone through anything as difficult as what I was going through now. I shared with the church the devastation of receiving news of my terminal cancer back in February and being told I had a short time to live. Here I was, six months later, on vacation with my four sons.

I told them I had put my faith completely in God, and that I was still alive and seeing great results through my treatment, all thanks to God. I explained that the only reason I was on vacation and at church was that God was working not only on my health but also on me, spiritually. He was building my faith. I had to trust God 100 percent. That meant I wouldn't worry, stress out or cry about my situation. I was to pray to Him, to trust Him and enjoy every day that He allowed me to open my eyes and live again, no matter what my circumstances were. I was no longer controlled by my emotions but by my faith. I felt free—free to vacation, free to enjoy my life, free to do anything. I truly felt like the clock was ticking and I couldn't waste time trying to solve my problems, so I let God take care of those things.

I let them know that life is short; that there is no time for negativity. You know the saying "Let go, and let God." Most of the time we let go and give God our problems, but if He doesn't fix them fast enough for us, we lose our patience and take the problems back and try to fix them ourselves. We wind up stressed out and worrying again with the same hopeless problems dragging us down.

As Hebrews 11:1 says, "Faith shows the reality of what we hope for; it is the evidence of things we cannot see." To have 100 percent faith we need to have 100 percent trust; not even 99 percent will be enough. There can't be any doubt. James 1:6-8 says "But when you ask, you must believe and not doubt, because the one who doubts is like a wave of the sea, blown and tossed by the wind. [7]That person should not expect to receive anything from the Lord. [8]Such a person is double-minded and unstable in all they do."

The congregation had a great response to the message. After the service there was a long line of people wanting to speak to me and thank me for sharing my testimony. It touched many people. A lady told me, "You're a walking miracle." People thanked me over and over. A gentleman said, "We read about miracles in the Bible, but to see one today, in front of us, is amazing!" As I spoke to my brothers and sisters, I realized everyone was going through tough situations in life, and the message helped them see that their problems weren't as big as they'd thought. Most compared their problems to what I was going through and were humbled for stressing or worrying about something so insignificant. The message was a big faith booster. Some people were in tears, realizing the time they had wasted on certain situations and problems. The message had opened their eyes and they felt liberated; they wanted to no longer worry or stress over small problems. Some said they were going to practice their faith; begin to pray and trust that God would take care of their problems. The church members encouraged me greatly through their words and through the love they demonstrated with all their hugs. Taking time out of my vacation to visit the church was a great decision for all involved. It was as encouraging for me as it was for them.

FINAL THOUGHT

This trip was very special. The time I spent with my boys was awesome! I will never forget this father-and-son time. We laughed, we drank, we ate and we bonded, and I will be eternally grateful to God for this time. Sharing my testimony at church was one of the most encouraging moments of my life.

My prayer: God, thank you for another day of life and for the incredible experiences on this trip. God, please open doors for me to share my testimony with the world. To be able to bring hope where there is no hope, to give faith to the faithless. To inspire and lead the way for people to connect with you. Amen.

BEING JOYFUL IN HOPE

ROMANS 12:12

Be joyful in hope, *patient in affliction, faithful in prayer.*

Chapter Six

GLIMMERS OF HOPE

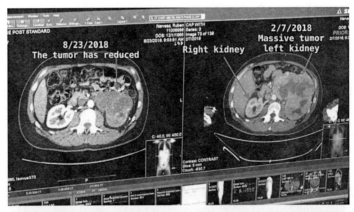

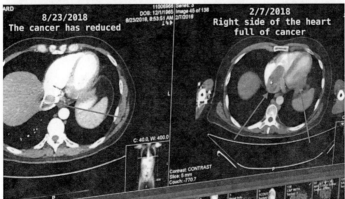

CT scan images of the heart and kidney comparing the scans from 2/7/2018 vs. 8/23/2018 (amazing shrinkage in 6 months).

EPHESIANS 1:19-20
*I also pray that you will understand the INCREDIBLE
GREATNESS of GOD'S POWER for us who believe him.
This is the same MIGHTY POWER that raised Christ
from the dead and seated him in the place of honor
at God's right hand in the heavenly realms.*

As the months went by, something incredible started to happen: the tumors began to shrink quite a bit. My doctor was surprised. "The cancer doesn't normally shrink that much and that fast," she said. "It's pretty amazing!"

Every CT scan I did after that was miracle after miracle. The tumors in the lungs were a lot smaller, the thrombus that grew through the vena cava into half of the heart had shrunk almost completely out of the heart and now was sitting at the entrance. It started to look like surgery may finally be an option.

In March of 2019 I had a CT scan done and it showed the cancer had stopped shrinking and stood stable. I met with my doctors, and they said that usually when the medicine stops working, it's time to switch treatments. There comes a point where the cancer learns how the medicine works, and it begins to fight off the effects from the medicine and can start to grow again. At my next appointment, my doctor felt this was time to have my surgery.

He said, "It's still going to be a very big and challenging surgery, but I think now is our time to start planning for it. It is a risky surgery; the biggest risk is bleeding. Sometimes with a surgery like this, we cut into the vein that carries all of the blood to the heart, and sometimes we can't control the bleeding and people do die in this type of surgery.

"Another thing that can happen is that when we stop the blood from going back to the heart, you have less blood flowing through your body. Sometimes the heart doesn't like it, and sometimes the brain doesn't like it, so things like a stroke or a heart attack can happen. Or a piece of the thrombus breaks off and goes into the lung and causes a pulmonary embolism.

"There are also other risks like injury to other organs like the intestine, spleen or the liver, risk of getting scar tissue in the abdomen, causing a bowel obstruction, or risk of a hernia in one of the incisions. There's always a chance that we open you up and we look, and we say we can't safely remove it.

"Before we can do a surgery like this, you need to see the anesthesiologist, have some bloodwork done and do an EKG. A surgery like this is usually at least six hours but sometimes takes eight, ten or twelve hours. Recovery: you're going to have a big incision, so it's going to be a long recovery. You are going to be in the hospital approximately five days, but some people are in the hospital longer. There's always a risk of complications; you might wind up back in the hospital with an infection or dehydration or something like that.

"After you leave the hospital, expect to be tired, worn out and sore. It's going to take around six weeks to get better."

I told the doctor I was going to talk to my family and see what we decided. At this point I was scared, and after hearing of all the ways I might die during surgery, I was terrified. I decided to talk with my wife and kids to get their input.

We met up the next day and I played a recording of my appointment for them. I told them I thought we should wait and do another three months of treatment. They all said, "It's time. If the doctor is recommending to do it, you should."

My family helped me a lot. They reminded me of my words about having faith, trusting God and not having fear. After hearing all of their input, my fear went away, and my faith came back. Listening to their encouragement and reminding me of the Scriptures all brought me back to a place that I needed to be: in God's care.

I called my doctor and said, "Let's do it, I'm in for the surgery." I went in for the pre-surgery requirements. The surgery was scheduled for May but one of the heart surgeons was unavailable, so they rescheduled for June 24.

FINAL THOUGHT

It's amazing how quickly we can lose faith when we are under pressure. Our own knowledge and strength are limited; God's power and knowledge are unlimited. If we lose faith, we stand alone and are doomed. I learned an important lesson in practicing my faith: Faith needs to be practiced at all times, and I need to make sure I never let fear creep in. Faith and fear do not exist together. Faith makes miracles happen.

Chapter Seven

GOING UNDER

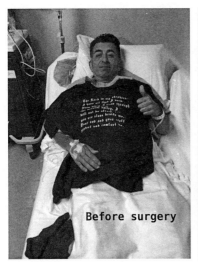
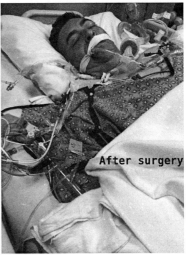

Before surgery and in ICU after surgery in a coma for 3 days.

PSALMS 23:4
Even when I walk through the darkest valley, I will not be
afraid, for you are close beside me.
Your rod and your staff protect and comfort me.

The day for surgery arrived. I woke up very early that morning; got ready, prayed and then my wife and I were on our way to the hospital. As we were driving, fear crept back in. I wondered if I would make it through the surgery. What complications might there be? Was it the right choice? Would I ever see my kids again?

My mind was thinking too fast and was out of control. My wife listened and suggested we pray on our drive; after all, the hospital was an hour away. We prayed but I still was uneasy.

I put on some worship music, then "Anchor for the Soul" by J. Brian Craig came on from my playlist. I turned it up and played it over and over. The words pierced my heart and mind, and it brought me so much peace.

I had prayed plenty leading up to the surgery, and I was already at peace with God and was ready to go home with Him if that was to be the outcome. I knew I couldn't go into surgery afraid; I needed to go in totally calm. It never fails; Satan will always try to confuse us with fear and negative thoughts. Thank God for worship music. The lyrics calmed me down completely.

We arrived at the hospital at 5:00 a.m. with friends and family waiting. With a big smile, I said, "I'm ready!" After greeting everyone, I checked in and they took me inside to my room.

As I waited with my wife by my bedside, my doctor came in, and several people came through to wish me luck. The last people to come through were Joel and Rocio Serna. We took a moment to pray and off they all went to the waiting room. It would be a long day for all of us.

The nurses took me into the surgery room, connected me to the IV and started with the anesthesia. The nurse said, "Count backward from ten." Ten . . . nine . . . and I was out. During the surgery I remember a point where I was being carried. I tried to see but I was in total darkness.

As fear tried to creep in, I remembered the Scripture from Psalms 23:4: "Even when I walk through the darkest valley, I will not be afraid, for you are close beside me. Your rod and your staff protect and comfort me." It was such a comforting moment knowing that God was carrying me through.

The surgery went well. I survived. Thank God! After ten hours of surgery, it was over. The doctors removed my left kidney, and they were able to remove the cancer that was in the vena cava and what was left in the heart. They placed me in a coma for three days for recovery.

There was a point while I was in a coma that I felt my throat was so dry I thought I was going to die. I couldn't scream, move or say anything since I was heavily sedated and intubated. My mind was conscious, and all I could think was, *I survived this surgery only to die from having lack of water*? It was torture and nerve-racking; it was horrible to be incapacitated. I thought, *If I make it out alive I'm going to sue this hospital for making me go through this torture*. It was really frightening.

When I finally was awakened, I heard the nurse tell my family that I was waking up. I saw my daughters, my wife, my sons and my sister around the bed. I tried to motion with my hand to my mouth, so they all started guessing at what I was trying to say: "Your mouth hurts?" "Do you want something?" My daughter put a tablet in front of me so I could type what I was trying to say but as I tried to type my hand was like spaghetti; because of the medicine, I had no control and couldn't push the letters that I wanted to so I went back to signaling.

They finally said "Water?" "YES!" Tears ran down my face; I was finally going to get some water to quench my thirst. I had been so desperate to hydrate my throat. All I could think was, *I'm not going to die after all*. The nurse said I couldn't have water but gave me some ice chips. At that moment it was like seeing steak and lobster. What a relief, once I got some ice chips down. I went through a few small cups of ice chips and was able to calm down. Later in the day they took me to my room, and I continued resting.

FINAL THOUGHT

It is incredible to know that I survived the surgery and that I am still alive. God does it again! The experience of being in a coma for three days was mind-blowing. Although I was out and couldn't feel anything, I was conscious. I had thoughts. Me being carried through the darkness, my dry throat, the thought of suing the hospital, ha ha ha.

I remembered those things when I woke up. In my mind I thought it was the same day as the surgery, not knowing three days had passed. I am grateful to be alive.

Chapter Eight

NEW REVELATIONS

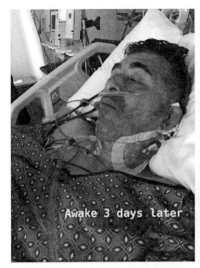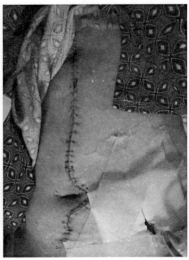

Awake in the hospital room. The incision from the surgery.

EXODUS 9:16
But I have spared you for a purpose—to show you my power and to spread my fame throughout the earth.

I was finally awake and conscious. I was able to see the many tubes stuck to my body. Tubes coming from my neck, my arms, my abdomen, several machines around my bed and nonstop hospital staff coming through. With my family around me, reality sank in: I'm alive! I'm alive!

Tears, tears and more tears. I was overjoyed to be alive. I thanked God, remembering Psalms 23. I thanked my family for their support. I thanked the nurses, the doctors and anyone who came through my room. I was ecstatic.

My family shared some tidbits of what had happened. I was shocked when they told me I had been in a coma for three days. I felt like it was the same day of the surgery. The different nurses that came through would say hello and make comments like, "Hey you, miracle man"; "Oh, this is the guy"; "I heard about you." I was thinking, *What are they talking about?*

Their comments were a little confusing to me—that is, until my doctor came to visit. He came in and asked how I was feeling. He then sat on my bed and said, "You must have a really strong will to live." He said the surgery lasted ten hours. "You lost fourteen units of blood and the trauma your body took! It's a miracle that you're alive. It's nothing I did. I can't take any credit; I just did my job." Then he started to explain the surgery details.

"I feel your surgery was a success. We were able to remove the kidney along with the big tumor. We were able to remove the thrombus from the vena cava and what was left in the heart, so you no longer have cancer in those areas except for the cancer in your lungs."

Great news! I was overwhelmed with gratitude toward God. As Psalms 23 says, He carried me through my darkest valley. I didn't fear. He was close beside me. I felt Him the whole time; I felt Him carry me. His staff and His rod guided and protected me.

During my surgery, there were moments of consciousness. In some of these moments I saw darkness. I felt anxiety and desperation. Someone was carrying me and I couldn't move. I was stiff; I wanted to cry. I felt helpless, but at the same time I felt peace.

Now came time for recovery. I could feel the soreness and pain from the surgery, which they controlled with pain pills and medicine through my IV. I tried to not take them, and that was a huge mistake. Once I felt the excruciating pain, I called the nurse and asked for relief. They got the pain under control pretty quickly.

My kidney was having trouble; since I'd been in a coma for a few days, my one and only kidney had stopped functioning. They tried a few procedures, but no luck. My doctor said they were going to have to put me on dialysis in hopes of getting my kidney to react and start working.

The doctor said, "If your kidney doesn't react, you may have to stay on dialysis permanently." The technician connected me to the machine and started the dialysis. It was one of the most painful procedures I have ever gone through, aside from my surgery.

After a few days of dialysis, my kidney finally started working. What a relief it was when the doctor said my kidney function was getting better, and after about a week they stopped the dialysis.

FINAL THOUGHT

The dialysis was very painful for me. I was connected for hours, and while I was on the machine, I would squirm from the pain. It caused me a lot of anxiety, but it was something I needed to do to get my kidney to work. I prayed constantly that it would work; I didn't want to stay on dialysis. Thank God that after a few days it was over. It was an experience I will never forget.

Chapter Nine

FLYING SOLO

Traveling solo in Guadalajara.

E C C L E S I A S T E S   3 : 1 2 – 1 3
*So I concluded there is nothing better than to be
happy and enjoy ourselves as long as we can. And
people should eat and drink and enjoy the fruits
of their labor, for these are gifts from God.*

In March of 2019, a few months before my surgery, I had taken a trip by myself to Guadalajara, Jalisco. A year had passed since my first infusion, my surgery was coming up and I was feeling somewhat anxious and felt I needed to get away and clear my mind. I was having negative thoughts on how much time I might have left to live, so I didn't want to stick around at home.

At home, I was inside most of the time. Everyone would go to work, and I would stay home. You can only watch so many movies and TV shows; it had gotten old, now that a year had passed. When I went out, I wore a face mask to protect myself from any illnesses I might contract since my immune system was weakened from my treatment. I spent lots of time exploring and planning the places I wanted to travel in Mexico. Everyone was working and busy, so I decided to go by myself this time.

My wife thought I was crazy going alone. She said, "What if you get sick out there? What if something happens?" I was thinking, *What if I'm not alive next month or next year? What if the cancer gets worse and I wind up in the hospital? I might not have this opportunity later; I just want to enjoy myself while I can.* She was a little worried, but my mind was set. I had to go. I wanted to travel, so I planned a quick two-day getaway to run around, with nothing or no one to hold me back.

I found a round-trip plane ticket for less than $100. I bought my ticket, packed a quick bag and I was off. It was a piece of cake traveling alone. Although I took a red-eye flight, as I got off the plane I was excited to begin my trip. When I landed in Guadalajara, it brought back memories from the last time I was there, when I was only ten years old. What I remember most is the Fiesta del Pueblo, lots of fireworks, fun, food and me riding a donkey around town all day. I'll never forget the feeling when I got off the donkey. I was sore for a while. I always considered that my first car.

All around the whole country of Mexico, every pueblo (small town) has their fiesta. Everyone in the pueblo attends; it's a time for families to gather and celebrate. Everyone decorates their houses. They hang colorful paper cutouts, running from house to house, across the streets, and as you walk the streets, it looks beautiful. Most fiestas have carnival rides. There is lots of food and desserts, and fireworks abound. There is usually a tall castillo (tower) built, layered with fireworks tied together. When the fuse is lit, it starts at the bottom and works its way up to the top, lighting every firework attached to the tower. It's an awesome spectacle. Toros (bulls) made of paper-mache and covered in fireworks are built like a tower with handles below. People run around holding the toros above their head and chase people as if the bull were charging at them. The toros shoot sparks in all directions, and if one gets close to you, it can burn your clothes or your skin. So you'd better run if a toro is coming toward you.

I went to where I was going to stay—a large, beautiful hacienda that I had rented a room in. I was the only one staying there, so I had the place all to myself and wow, this place was amazing! I dropped off my suitcase, changed and was off to start my two-day stay in Guadalajara. The first place I wanted to visit was Tlaquepaque. I walked Calle Independencia, where there are a lot of restaurants, shops and art throughout the area. You can spend quite a while browsing through the shops and stopping to taste all of the treats and drinks along the way. When in Guadalajara, you have to eat birria, which is one of the foods they are famous for.

I walked over to the center of Tlaquepaque, to El Parian. El Parian is a square in which there are many restaurants, bars and live music, mostly mariachi music. As I got closer, I could smell the food, and the smell was making me hungry. As I walked in, I saw the fresh tortillas being made by hand and the chefs in the kitchen cooking up a storm. There are quite a few restaurants to choose from and the hosts have menus in hand, all waving you into their restaurant.

Since it was a weekday and I had arrived early, there weren't many people, so I was a popular guy. I sat down, ordered my birria plate and had a drink while I listened to some great music. The birria was delicious, as expected: juicy, tender and so flavorful, I could eat this every day. I left the restaurant, bought some souvenirs and left. From there I went to Tonala.

In Tonala, there are many artesanos who have their shops where you can buy many different types of handmade artistry. Wooden, metal, ceramic and glass items, paintings, furniture and so on. As I walked the streets, I found some art I really liked. I brought back a piece of aluminum artwork depicting an Aztec and an Aztec eagle. I also bought four ceramic figures—a male and female mariachi along with a couple of figures of Mexican women. I picked up several other art pieces to add to my collection.

The host at my hacienda recommended a great seafood restaurant in Tonala called El Arandense, so I had to try it. Here I was, eating again and listening to more live music. I ordered a shrimp cocktail and a fish plate. The food was delicious, and now I was really stuffed. I relaxed there for a while and enjoyed the music. After that, I went to downtown Guadalajara to stroll around and see the many historic and colonial buildings in the area. On my way there, I noticed some incredible architecture. There were a few nice bridges and some amazing buildings— this was a big, beautiful city.

It was a nice, relaxing quick trip, and I got to explore a little bit of Guadalajara but I was left wanting more of this city, so I would definitely have to come back. There are still a few cities I need to explore. The obvious one is Tequila, so I can do a tequila tasting tour and explore the distilleries. I would also like to visit Cocula, the city where the first mariachi band was born. It's the crib of mariachi music. Chapala is another city I want to visit–there is a big lake and some great restaurants there. I went as a young boy, but I'm sure it has changed a lot by now.

What an amazing experience. I felt rejuvenated, happy and clear-headed. Not once did I think about the cancer or hold back for any reason; I felt free. Another incredible adventure on the books. Well, it was time to go home, get some rest and prepare for my next infusion. It was nice to be alone, but I missed my family. I don't know what's coming in the future, in regard to my health; it's pretty scary, but I am definitely going to keep traveling as long as I am physically able. God, I can't thank you enough. I may be dying, but I'm ready for anything.

FINAL THOUGHT

It's amazing what a few days of travel can do for your mental health. How much joy and excitement are waiting for us if we just take that step. Sometimes the best trips are the spur-of-the-moment, unplanned ones, where you leap into the unknown. There were concerns and doubts, but the desire to travel overcame everything. I am glad I chose to go; no regrets there.

Being alone let me think clearly; I had no other opinions. I got to enjoy myself; I made myself happy. I was able to do what I like–to stop or go where I wanted at any moment. I will definitely have to do it again and make it a longer stay. In addition to chemotherapy, I consider traveling as my other therapy; it illuminates my life tremendously.

BEING PATIENT IN AFFLICTION

ROMANS 12:12

Be joyful in hope, **patient in affliction***, faithful in prayer.*

Chapter Ten

GET UP AND WALK

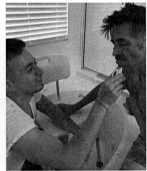

(Top Images) My son Andy bathing me and giving me a shave.
(Image Center) A few months later in a wheelchair,
at Six Flags with my wife, Rosalba.

JOHN 5:8
Jesus told him, "Stand up, pick up your mat, and walk!"

After a long grueling surgery, lots of drugs and treatments that kept me lying in my hospital bed for two weeks, now it was time to begin working toward walking. This was a requirement if I wanted to go home. I had to be able to eat, poop and walk.

Still in a lot of pain, with the help of the physical therapist, my son Andy and a walker, I stood up from my hospital bed. I slowly walked to the restroom then took a short walk through the hall. What a challenge—I was really tired after that. Who would imagine such a simple task would be so difficult? Little did I know it would be months before I would be able to walk on my own.

I finally left the hospital a few days later. Once I arrived at home, my son Gabriel carried me in his arms upstairs to my bedroom and the challenge to become mobile began. Having to go to the restroom was tough—although it was only a short walk, the strength it took wore me out.

My first bath was humbling. My wife turned on the heater and got towels and my clean clothes ready. My son Andy set the mood. He put on some classic reggae music and began to work. Andy, along with my wife, undressed me, then carried me into the bathtub where a chair was waiting for me to sit in. I couldn't lift my leg high enough to climb into the tub and because of the surgery, I couldn't sit in the tub; I still had gauze covering my wounds where I once had tubes stuck in me.

As Andy poured water on my head and body, I shivered quite a bit. As he scrubbed my body, I began to weep. I cried and cried; I was overwhelmed with emotion. I was like an infant unable to care for myself. I couldn't fathom not being able to bathe myself; I had no strength or balance. I wasn't sure if this was how life would be from now on, and I felt it was burdensome, but my wife and son kept saying, "It's okay; we're here to help you, You're going to be fine; this is temporary."

I thanked them over and over with tears in my eyes. "THANK YOU! THANK YOU!" It was such an emotional moment, it was unforgettable. These are the moments I most treasure in my life.

At first, I needed help getting in and out of bed and walking to the restroom. After a couple of days, I began walking to the restroom using a walker. After about a week or so, I was able to walk around my bedroom with the walker, and soon I was able to walk all the way into the loft. Although it was a short walk, I felt like I had done a marathon.

I continued to practice walking daily and after about another month passed, I began to work on going up and down the stairs. It took several days, and after a few attempts, I could finally do it. Holding on tight to the rails and using all of my strength, I made it up the stairs and walked to my room. It was nice to see and visit the downstairs of my house, to sit at the dinner table and in our living room. How I had missed the liberty of walking through my house.

I had a physical therapist come in a couple of times a week to teach me some exercises to strengthen my legs and arms. I used bands to work out and the process helped me a lot to get back into walking shape. It took me another month to confidently walk around. I mostly walked around like a zombie with my arms stretched out in front of me, reaching for things to hold on to and to pull myself up. It took me about three months to finally be able to walk semi-normally again; no running, but I could walk without assistance.

Now when we go shopping, I sometimes park as far as I can from the front entrance. This works twofold: you don't have to wait or fight for a parking spot, and you can walk a little extra to get some exercise. What a blessing it is to have legs and to use them, whether it's to walk or run. We sometimes take those small things for granted. No more wheelchairs and no more walkers; I'm walking again, and I can't wait to drive.

FINAL THOUGHT

In life, we really take things for granted. Our arms, legs, eyes and so on seem like normal things. When we lose them, we realize how blessed we are to have them, how useless we are without them, how much we really depend on them and how much we need them. I am truly grateful for my life but most of all I am grateful just to be living, no matter the circumstances. To simply be alive is incredible. Enjoy the simple things in life: sunsets, walks, sitting on the porch—all of that is free.

Chapter Eleven

TRIALS OF MANY KINDS

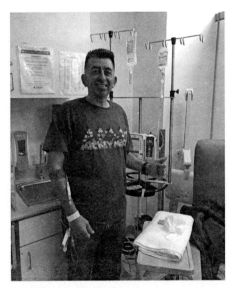

Infusion day.

JOHN 10:10
The thief's purpose is to steal and kill and destroy.
My purpose is to give them a rich and satisfying life.

The enemy—the devil—tried again to steal my joy, rob me of my faith, destroy my faith that I have in my almighty God.

Today I was bullied and beaten up by the devil and his demons. Left battered and bruised, hurt and in inconsolable pain.

After some great success with my treatment and surgery, I was convinced that my cancer battle was soon coming to an end. They had removed the bulk of the cancer, and now all I had were tumors in both lungs. *Piece of cake*, I thought. I went in for my next infusion on August 15, 2019, and I went back in September for another one, but wound up hospitalized. My potassium was really high, and I was in danger of having a stroke, so my doctor had me skip the infusion.

In October, I came in for my infusion and also did a CT scan. This was the first scan since my surgery. When they injected the contrast through the IV, I had a reaction and began vomiting, so the techs did the CT scan without contrast. After that experience of having thrown up all over my clothes, I bring extra clothes to every CT scan; I want to be prepared in case it happens again.

I did my monthly infusions for the next couple of months and did another CT scan in January. The news was not what I expected; I was caught completely by surprise, partially my fault for second-guessing the devil's schemes. The devil knows who my God is, which is why at times it puzzles me that the devil would even try to win. He's ALWAYS going to lose.

When the doctor gave me the results of my CT scan, I was left without words. To hear that I now had two new tumors in my right lung, five new tumors in my left lung, and to top it off, that the tumors I already had had grown double and triple in size—was a lot to bear. The cancer was growing out of control.

Here I had arrived expecting that my treatment of two years was almost over, and now the doctors were recommending switching me to a different treatment. I was about to start all over again and begin taking a dose of chemo pills daily rather than infusions every four weeks. This drug was stronger, with more side effects. It was another experiment to try and stop the growth, at least, and maybe even shrink the tumors.

I realized this was another battle in the war against the cancer that had been trying to kill me. I had to confront and win this battle. The victory felt close, but it had slipped away (for now). It was a setback, you might say. My only weapon was prayer and also my faith that God would carry me to victory!

The best part was, I knew that I was not alone. The support of my family and the army of friends who were fighting alongside me was incredible! How could I possibly lose?

With cancer, you just never know. One day you're making progress and then another day it's growing like wildfire. Satan wants to kill my faith, destroy my hope and ruin my future. All of these problems and strife come from the devil; he wants to discourage us at all times. He wants us to fear; he wants us to lose heart.

This whole cancer situation I'm going through is not from God; it is from the devil, and he's angry! He can't win so he throws smoke bombs—all types of distractions—but we have to stay focused. We have to sit still, pray and trust that God is working at all times.

God has plans: Jeremiah 29:11 says, "'For I know the plans I have for you,' declares the Lord, 'plans to prosper you and not to harm you, plans to give you hope and a future.'"

I believe with all my heart that this is true: plans "not to harm you"; therefore my situation is not from God. He has spared me, and for that I am grateful.

To God be the glory!

FINAL THOUGHT

James 1:2 says, "Consider it pure joy, my brothers and sisters, whenever you face trials of many kinds."

You never know what is going to happen next in your life. One moment everything is going great, and the next moment, you're facing a life-or-death situation. It's easy to be happy when things are going well; we feel blessed. The challenge is to have the same emotion and attitude when things are at their worst in our lives. To have faith—to trust that God is with us and is in full control of our situation. Always pray. Be joyful always!

Chapter Twelve

SURRENDERING

Ruben and Rosalba at one of the hospital appointments.

PHILIPPIANS 1:21
For to me, living means living for Christ,
and dying is even better.

My heart was still mending from the news I had received a few weeks prior. My faith had not left me. I trusted God would protect me and do His will. Similar to Paul's words in Philippians, I was personally convinced, nothing would separate me from the love of my God!

One afternoon I received the chemo pills, so I made a plan to start taking them the next day. When I woke up the next morning, I knew I had to pray before taking my first dose and prepare myself before diving into this new chemo treatment.

My wife and I knelt down to pray; we gave this whole situation to God. Tears began to flow as we cried out to God; our emotions connected with our Father's heart. We thanked Him for His forgiveness and for so many blessings. We praised Him. We both lay our worries before Him, the reality of what we felt; we confided our innermost feelings.

What an amazing feeling! Casting our cares to God, our faith was enlightened, our hearts and minds were at peace. We found the tranquility to move forward and to trust that God would continue to work through this medicine.

Thank you, God! We wait to see more miracles done by your hands and through your strength.

After a few weeks, the majority of my hair starts to turn gray, my facial hair is completely gray and I begin to struggle with hand and foot syndrome. My feet turn a bright red and start to have blisters on their underside, which prevents me from being able to walk. The side effects at times are unbearable. My doctor suggests lowering the dose, so they switch me to a lower dose. The side effects continue, so I take breaks to let the effects wear off, and as they come back, I continue to take breaks.

Around eight months have passed on this new treatment. Today I go in for another CT scan to see what the results are from these chemo pills I've been on. My oncologist comes in and she goes over the results with me.

She says the scan shows the cancer has spread to the pelvic wall, to the colon (small and large intestines), to the liver vessel, to the left pulmonary artery and to the psoas muscle. My doctor suggests adding infusions every four weeks again as part of my treatment to hopefully help stop it from spreading any further.

I agree, and so begins another chapter with infusions. God has moved bigger mountains; I'm excited to see what miracles God does, moving forward.

The following month when I go in for my infusion, my doctor is out so my appointment is with another oncologist from her team. We go over my labs, and he goes over my medical history.

He tells me, "You know that your prognosis is terminal, correct?"

"Yes," I say.

"You've been on this treatment for two and a half years now. You know that for people on this treatment, their life expectancy is three years?"

He explains to me specifically what the medicine does. He says, "This medicine you're getting restricts your blood flow. That's good because it slows down the growth of the cancer but it also restricts the blood flow to your organs and that causes damage to your organs that eventually will cause them to fail. So the medicine does some good things but it also does some bad things. Enjoy your life, sir. You could be looking at your last six months of life."

I tell him that I enjoy every day of life that God gives me. I explain to him how much I travel and that I take many trips locally too. I tell him, "You know, I live like I don't have cancer. I don't give the thought a second in my mind. Every day is an adventure for me."

He laughs and says, "You have the right attitude. It was great meeting you. Enjoy your day."

When hearing those types of things, like "You're going to die within the next six months," I give those things to God. I tell Him, "God, did you hear what he said? Okay great, you take care of that." I can't change it; I don't have any control. Worrying or stressing over those words won't help me. They could paralyze me if I paid any attention to them.

I've got a life to enjoy; on to my next adventure.

FINAL THOUGHT

Bad news seems never-ending. The end seems near. Cancer is so unpredictable. You've got to just laugh; what else can you do? I've got to stay positive and remember that I am alive. I can enjoy today. I can walk, I can see; I can do many things. I have to keep that negative news out of my mind. I am a blessed man. I choose my faith. God will fix it; He always does.

Chapter Thirteen

SONS AND MOTHERS

My mom Maria and me, at the Shrine of Christ
the King (El Cubilete) in Silao, Guanajuato.

EPHESIANS 6:3
*If you honor your father and mother, "things will go well
for you, and you will have a long life on the earth."*

A year prior, at the end of October 2019, I was feeling pretty good physically from my surgery and was able to drive. I planned a nine-day trip with my mom so we could spend some quality time together. I had brought her out to Mexico before but there had been eleven other family members who had come along. This time, I wanted to get some mom-and-son time in and have my mom all to myself. I thought it would be a good time for us to talk and enjoy each other's company and see the very popular Dia de los Muertos parade in Mexico City. We had a great time touring the city. Everywhere was decorated with Dia de los Muertos décor, flowers, posters, altars and so on.

When we arrived at the parade route it was raining, and my mom said she didn't want to get wet—that she would wait in the car while I went and watched the parade in the rain. I wasn't going to watch the parade by myself, so I decided to go to Puebla instead since the weather looked better out there. We arrived in Puebla, and our first stop was to eat some mole. My mom had been wanting to eat mole since our last trip, and here we were, finally. As she ate, she had a big smile on her face. "This mole is delicious," she said. "Finally I get to eat mole in Puebla." We enjoyed our dinner and went out to the streets to walk around. The city was jumping.

There was a concert in the plaza and the band Los Estramboticos was playing. As we walked by, their song "Peter Punk" came on and everyone started jumping up and down. We stood there and listened to the music for a bit, then went and had dessert. While eating our dessert, we stood and saw a kids' band playing songs in front of the cathedral. They played a lot of classic Mexican songs and entertained the crowd. My mom loved the mini concert. The songs they played reminded her of when she was young; she was reminiscing and singing along to the music. We finished up and went to our room. Once we were in our room, she said, "That was fun!" She couldn't stop telling me how good the mole was and how close a drive it was from Mexico City. She went on and on about all of the things we had done that day. I was so glad my mom was enjoying this trip as much as me.

The next day, we walked the city looking at the altars that were on display for Dia de los Muertos. We walked through the art district, where I bought some art, and we went to an art exhibition in one of the plazas. We left there and headed to Cholula, where we saw a Dia de los Muertos parade and took pictures with several girls dressed as Catrinas. We stopped to eat at one of my favorite places in Cholula, El Ancla y la Sirena. I had my mom try an empanada, and then we both ate shrimp soup (caldo de camarones). "That's one of the best caldos I've ever tasted," she said.

"I know; that's why I brought you here. I love this place," I told her.

We left to go back to Mexico City and spent the night there. On our drive, we talked about our family. I asked her about my great-grandparents, my grandparents and other family members from Mexico. I always liked to go over our family tree with her and hear stories about what it was like when she was young. The next day we went to church. I was speaking that day, so it was great to have my mom by my side. After service, I introduced my mom to many of my friends. "Your son is an inspiration," a lady told her. "What a blessing it is to have you and your son here; thank you for visiting us." My mom received so many greetings and kind words. She was really impacted by the love and attention we got. It was an unforgettable experience; a huge blessing. From there, we went to have dinner with my friends Marcelo and Marco, and their families.

The next day we drove to Queretaro, and on our way we stopped to eat barbacoa at one of my favorite places just outside the city. After breakfast, we did some sightseeing and spent the day in Queretaro. In the early afternoon, I took her to a really nice restaurant. She was impressed with the décor and the ambience of the restaurant, especially the food. She was taking pictures of everything and admiring the art on the walls, the chandeliers and the décor. We ate and left the city for our next stop, Leon, Guanajuato.

On our drive, I took a moment to express some feelings of regret I had from my teen years and as an adult. Although we had talked about it before, it was in my heart to apologize to my mom for my rebelliousness. I told her I was really sorry for disrespecting her and for the hurt I had caused her. Now that I have older kids, I realize the pain you sometimes go through, raising kids, and it makes you remember what type of son or daughter you were.

She was quick to stop me and said, "It's okay, mijo, it's in the past. I forgive you." Her words were comforting. I know she loves me and that it's in the past, but it was on my heart to remind her that I was sorry for all the pain I had caused her. My mom has been through a lot in her life, and I wanted her to feel some comfort and know that I was there for her, as she has been for me. I know she still worries for me; I can't imagine what a parent feels, knowing that their child has cancer. But here we were, vacationing together and making memories. What a blessing to spend time with my mom.

We arrived, had a late dinner and then were off to rest in our room. The next day after breakfast, we went to see a beautiful neo-Gothic church called Templo Expiatorio del Sagrado Corazon de Jesus. It was built from 1921 to 2013—it took ninety-two years to build. It has a resemblance to Notre Dame cathedral. It has beautiful stained-glass windows and incredible arches inside the church. My mom was in awe; it was the first time she had seen this type of church.

A couple of blocks away is an arch that resembles the Arc de Triomphe in Paris, France, except this one has a lion on top and is much smaller. We walked around the area looking at all the statues and sculptures in the area. We left there and I took her to the Zona Piel, where they sell leather goods like jackets, shoes, purses and so on. My mom had been planning her day there and was excited to buy herself some leather goods. She bought a leather jacket, some gifts and some souvenirs. She was like a kid in a candy store, shopping for hours.

We went to dinner and back to our room. We made some coffee and talked for a while about the places we'd seen, the great food we'd eaten and the overall experience. She said, "It's only been a few days and we've already done so many things. Where else are we going?" We went over the plans for the next few days and then went to bed. She was like a child, all excited about the trip. As excited as she was, I'm sure she dreamed about our trip the whole night, or she didn't sleep at all from the excitement.

The next morning, we drove to Silao, Guanajuato, to the Cerro del Cubilete, a nice church that sits on a 660-foot mountain. It's one of the most historically religious shrines in Mexico. On top of the church, there is an 80-foot statue of Christ that weighs 80 tons. It is the largest Christ statue in the world made of bronze. The style of the church is art deco. The inside as well as the outside are beautiful; it's an incredible sight. We walked around for a bit, bought some souvenirs and left.

From there we drove to the centro historico de Guanajuato (the historic center of downtown Guanajuato), went to our hotel, dropped off our stuff and went on our way. We walked to the Callejon del Beso. From there we went to the Diego Rivera Museum and then we went to the Mummy Museum (Museo de las Momias). We went back to the centro and had dinner and then walked around the area to see the college and the Teatro Juarez. We ended our trip there and headed back the next day to Mexico City and flew back home. It was a bit tiring, but spending the time alone with my mom was awesome. Although we talk daily and see each other frequently to have breakfast or lunch, the time is always limited. On this trip, we had plenty of time to talk, to laugh and to experience so many things together.

FINAL THOUGHT

I am so grateful for this trip. My mom and I were able to bond like never before. The experience of traveling together was amazing, and I will cherish these moments forever. To see the joy in my mom's eyes, to hear her speak of the trip as the days passed. The conversations as we drove state to state. To see her face as she ate so many different foods; she got the full experience of Mexico. Several states, amazing events, all sorts of food and fun.

Thank you, God, for allowing me to spend this time with my mom and for my amazing recovery from surgery. For giving me my legs and arms to drive around, to walk and to enjoy this unforgettable trip without any hindrances.

BEING FAITHFUL IN PRAYER

ROMANS 12:12

Be joyful in hope, patient in affliction, **faithful in prayer**.

Chapter Fourteen

PRE-ANSWERED PRAYERS

Me at my monthly appointment, keeping the HOPE alive.

PSALMS 34:4
I prayed to the Lord, and he answered me.
He freed me from all my fears.

There are so many challenges to confront–physical, mental–and then there's the financial challenges. During this time, I received a bill for $8,800 for co-payments for my doctor visits. At first sight of the bill, I was overwhelmed; I felt like it was another burden to carry. How was I going to pay this? Where was I going to get this money? I hate owing money, and I don't like bills, especially medical bills.

I decided to not carry the weight of this debt and sincerely prayed that God would help me out with this. I didn't want it to be a distraction or cause any stress now that I was going to start my infusions again.

On May 21, we met with our Bible group and I told them about the letter I'd received and asked if we could pray for that bill to be somehow eliminated. It was hard for me to forget about that debt, and it was constantly in the back of my mind, since the hospital had called me a few times already trying to make payment arrangements.

We all prayed, spent some time together and then all went home. A couple of days later I went to go get my mail and I opened one of the letters. It was a letter from Squibb/Bristol Myers. First of all, the letter was dated May 20. The letter said that I had been accepted to receive help for co-payments related to my treatment. I would be covered for up to $25,000 for the whole year of services dating back from January 1 through December 31.

We prayed on the twenty-first and here this letter was dated the twentieth. God had already taken care of my worries. Now with my new insurance starting on July 1, this program would cover my past costs from January 1, and the future co-payments with the new insurance through the end of the year.

Who had enrolled me in this program? Who had had the idea of taking care of my debt? I had so many questions. The next time I went into the hospital for my doctor appointment I stopped by the financial office and showed the lady the letter.

She said, "Okay, it looks like Squibb will cover the costs of your co-payments. I'll apply it to your account." I asked her if someone in her office had enrolled me in the program and she said no—that she didn't have any idea who might have enrolled me.

Isn't it incredible how these things happen? Coincidence? Prayer is powerful! What gets me is that we prayed on the twenty-first and little did I know that the problem had already been solved.

God always wants us to cast our burdens on Him. He's able to do so much more; all we have to do is trust Him. It was another faith-building moment, not just for me but for everyone involved.

This isn't the first time God got me out of a financial jam. In the beginning of my cancer journey I had frozen shoulders for a few months before I went into the hospital. It was amazing that we were able to get by financially since I was unable to work for so long. We did raffles, my family and friends took in donations, and my friends, family and my church all donated for my financial needs. I was able to cover the insurance costs, medicine costs and co-payments when I started treatment. Everyone came together. I received so much love and support from all over. What's amazing is, God knew exactly how much money I needed. Just as the money ran out, my monthly income started to come in just in time to help continue covering the costs I now had. As the Scripture says in Philippians 4:6, "Don't worry about anything; instead, pray about everything. Tell God what you need, and thank him for all he has done."

FINAL THOUGHT

So many times, we worry about things that God has already taken care of or is working on resolving for us. We become impatient so quickly, but God wants us to always be patient and to trust Him. I have to trust that God is sending me help through these medicines.

He is always working, even when things take a turn for the worse; He will work it out for His glory. I have to keep in mind how powerful He is. Thank you, God, for always taking care of me and all of my problems.

Chapter Fifteen

ASKING BIGGER

Ruben and Rosalba at church after receiving
the call from the oncologist.

JOHN 11:40
*Jesus responded, "Didn't I tell you that you
would see God's glory if you believe?"*

I have seen God's glory once again. God is amazing and so powerful! An amazing miracle happened once again! God NEVER lets us down; we just have to believe.

I'm going to go back a couple of months to grasp the fullness of this miracle.

Back in August, one of my oncologists told me of a new clinical trial called CAR T cell treatment. It was just starting, and he wanted to get me a spot and asked if I was interested. I was pumped to try something new and said yes.

He interviewed me and went through my case and said I was definitely a good candidate. He said it would take around six months to get a spot for me, so just to be patient but that he would get me in.

A few months later on December 31, my insurance was canceled so I would have to stop my cancer treatment as the infusions cost around $80,000 every four weeks. The insurance company told me I now qualified for Medicare since I had been disabled for two years and that I needed to contact them. Trying to sign up was a nightmare, and after two months of trying, I was told I wouldn't have coverage until July.

During these two months I was unable to do my infusions, so I had no treatment. Initially there was some fear that without treatment the cancer would definitely grow, so when I got the news, I asked our family group at church (made up of five couples), "Can you join me and my wife in praying that God will hold back the cancer like He held the sun for Joshua (Joshua 10:12-14) and also ask Him to show us a sign of His power by shrinking it at least a little?"

After going back and forth trying to get insured, I got back on Covered CA (my regular insurance) but at three times the cost. Since I now qualified for Medicare, I no longer qualified for the subsidy. Oh well, I desperately needed insurance so I could get my treatment that has helped to keep me alive these last three years.

Fast-forward to March. I was by now insured again (thank God), so I went in for my infusion on March 11. On March 23, I got a call from my oncologist saying a spot had opened up for me for the new clinical trial. "I need you to come in tomorrow morning to do three cat scans, labs and then see me. I need the scans to confirm you qualify for the CAR T cell treatment."

To qualify, the cancer couldn't have metastasized to the brain and needed to show some growth. Since I hadn't done my infusions for almost three months, the scans should have shown some obvious growth, because my last infusion before March 11 was on December 17.

The next day the oncologist called me with the results and said the cancer was not in the brain and looked stable in the other areas. He asked if I still wanted to do the treatment, and I said yes.

We scheduled the appointment for April 24, 2021. On my way to church on Sunday, March 28, my oncologist called me and said, "I've got good news and bad news. The bad news is you don't qualify for the CAR T cell treatment. The good news is your cancer actually shrunk a little, so that disqualifies you. Congratulations!

We're not sure how that happened since you hadn't done any infusions in almost three months. I'll keep checking on you, and if the cancer grows, we'll definitely get you a seat for the trial."

We arrived at our church service, and I went in and shared the incredible news with my friends. I asked my friend and pastor Joel, "Do you remember what we were praying for?"

"Yeah, for your cancer to not grow and shrink at least a little," he said. I told him about the phone call, and he laughed and said, "Wow, we lacked faith—we should've asked God to remove it completely." We had a good laugh and were reminded of how powerful prayer and God are.

FINAL THOUGHT

The news of the cancer shrinking without treatment brings tears to my eyes. I am humbled and grateful. I am flabbergasted. Prayer definitely works. I am blown away at what God is able to do with a simple request, a prayer by His people.

What is really going on here? A miracle! God, thank you! I believe! Forgive me if I have ever doubted you. Mighty God of Heaven, I am in awe.

Chapter Sixteen

PRAYERS FROM PRISON

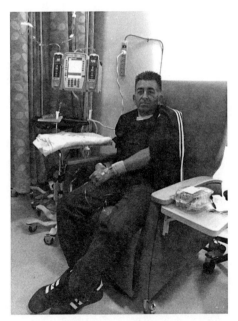

Ruben at the hospital.

Acts 16:31

They were severely beaten, and then they were
thrown into prison. The jailer was ordered
to make sure they didn't escape.

In Acts 16, the Apostle Paul and Silas are arrested and put in prison. They're stripped and severely beaten with wooden rods and then placed in the inner dungeon with their feet clamped in the stocks.

Around midnight, instead of sleeping or complaining of their injuries, they prayed and sang hymns to God.

All of the prisoners were listening to them, and suddenly an earthquake struck. The doors flew open and the chains of every prisoner fell off.

After all of the commotion, the jailer asks Paul and Silas, "Sirs, what must I do to be saved?" They share the good news of Jesus: "Believe, and you will be saved," they tell the jailer.

Obviously, it wasn't only the prisoners who were listening to Paul and Silas. The jailer was also listening to them when they were praying and singing. In Acts 16:23-34, the story says the jailer cared for their wounds, he brought them into his household and he set a meal before them. It also says his entire household rejoiced because they all believed in God, and they were all immediately baptized.

To me, Paul and Silas's example is amazing. While suffering and in prison, Paul continued to share the Gospel and worship God. He didn't complain; his life and purpose didn't change. While in prison, his relationship with God continued firmly. Not once did he curse Him or ask, *Why did you let them arrest me, God?* No, his faith stayed the same, or maybe grew stronger through this challenge.

I can relate to Paul being in jail with pain and suffering. I can also relate to his faith and glorifying God in all circumstances, no matter what the challenge.

For me, the hospital I visit every four weeks for my infusions is my prison. The nurses, doctors and office staff are the jailers, and the patients are prisoners in my eyes. This hospital is a big prison; the harvest is plenty.

On my way to my appointments, I listen to worship music, most of the time at full blast. I like to prepare my heart with music and prayer before I arrive. When I walk in, my focus is to hopefully touch someone with my testimony or to also have someone believe that there is a God.

I know most of the patients are all suffering in one way or another, some physically, many emotionally. My message to them is that there is still hope and that faith in God can and will always get you through anything. I always ask God for boldness and to guide me to the people He wants to touch.

In the last four years, I've shared with many patients and staff during my visits and have made some great friends, too. I've met people who are going through many emotions related to their prognosis. Some have bitterness and anger, and most also have a lot of fear; many times it's also the family members dealing with the emotions too. I've also met many people who have been in remission for many years; that is amazing.

Once I shared with one of my nurses, a nice Filipino lady. As I spoke, tears began running down her cheeks. She said, "How can you be so happy with all that you are going through?" She began to share her life and things she was going through. She realized her problems were so minuscule compared to mine. I shared about my travels and things I do, and she was blown away. She gave me her phone number and said she was going to tell her husband to take time off work and that they wanted to travel to Mexico with me.

One day while waiting to get my CT scan done, I was sharing with a gentleman whom I thought was a patient. I was telling him how I don't think about having cancer—that I don't give that thought a second in my mind, that I live as if I don't have cancer.

His wife was lying back in her chair, and all of a sudden she popped up and said, "How do you do that?! How do you not think about having cancer?!"

"I can't ignore my situation," I told her, "but just like Peter Pan says, 'Think happy thoughts.' I saw all my six children being born, so those are some of my happiest memories for me. Think of things like that," I told her. "You can remember a vacation, a birthday, a holiday gathering. I am sure you have happy memories that you can focus on instead of your illness." She wasn't too convinced, but I tried.

I met a nice man in his early seventies one day while we were waiting to see our doctors, and as we talked, we ran out of time. Once both of our appointments were over, we ran into each other again, so I invited him for lunch at the cafeteria so we could continue our conversation. He told me no one had ever asked him to have lunch, much less spend time with him. We almost fought over who would pay. I said, "I invited you." We went back and forth and I wound up gladly paying for our lunches. I told him, "You can get it next time."

We enjoyed our time together sharing our cancer stories and then went on to talk about our families and experiences. We spent a few hours together, exchanged numbers and a friendship began. We've met up for lunch a few more times and have stayed in touch.

I have made so many great friends and am making some great memories here in my prison. Most cancer patients fear death and for some like me with stage 4 terminal cancer, it is a reality; it is not something you can ignore. But my focus is on eternity and on what my future with God will be.

Of course, it pains me to think of someday not seeing my family anymore and also the pain and grief it will cause them when I pass. Those things are inevitable, and I consider them all the time, but meanwhile I will make the best of every day I have with them.

This life here on earth is temporary. Regarding life in heaven, Revelation 21:4 says: "He will wipe every tear from their eyes, and there will be no more sorrow or crying or pain. All these things are gone forever." Verse 7 says, "All who are victorious will inherit these blessings, and I will be their God and they will be my children." That inspires me. Those are things that comfort my soul, bring me peace and keep my focus on my eternal future.

I've learned that prison is not so bad if you're close to God and focused on your purpose. As Peter Pan says, "It is not in doing what you like, but in liking what you do that is the secret of happiness." I like what I do, serving God; He has the best benefits no company can offer.

I've been in prison for four years so far and I am not sure how long my sentence will be, but I will make the best of every visit. I will continue to pray for those whom God puts in my path. I pray for open hearts because as people go through these difficulties, their hearts become hardened and they are closed to God's message. God, please take away the feeling of being cursed or punished and open people's eyes to your calling. Let them see you are trying to bless them through their trials. Let me continue to encourage and give hope to everyone I come across.

FINAL THOUGHT

Every trial is difficult but can be a blessing. We need faith when challenges come our way. We need to relay the message in James 1:2-4: [2]Dear brothers and sisters, when troubles of any kind come your way, consider it an opportunity for great joy. [3]For you know that when your faith is tested, your endurance has a chance to grow. [4]So let it grow, for when your endurance is fully developed, you will be perfect and complete, needing nothing.

Chapter Seventeen

BROTHERS AND SISTERS

My brother Edward (Led), left, and me at the
O2 in London to see Robert Plant.

ECCLESIASTES 2:24–25
*So I decided there is nothing better than to enjoy food
and drink and to find satisfaction in work. Then I
realized that these pleasures are from the hand of God.
For who can eat or enjoy anything apart from him?*

At the end of September 2018, I took a trip with my wife to Mexico City. I planned to speak at a few of our churches on Sunday, September 30, and was also going to spend some time with my wife's family celebrating my mother-in-law's birthday. We flew out early on September 29, arrived and spent the day with our family. The next morning, we went to church to meet my friend Marco, and we drove to our church in Texcoco. I preached there and spent a little time with the members of our church.

It was nice to have my wife by my side. Before, I had come a few times and spoken at several churches, but I had come alone. So it was nice for people to get to know my wife and hear her perspective on dealing with my cancer situation. She gave great input and inspired many people with her faith as well. From there, we met with a group of leaders from another ministry and shared with them, and then we all ate together. We left there and went over to my mother-in-law's house as we were celebrating her seventy-ninth birthday. We arrived, and shortly afterward, the mariachi came in and played for a few hours while we all ate.

We went to bed after the party, and that night, I was awakened by extreme pain. I spent that night vomiting, with cold sweats and extreme pain in my abdomen. By the morning I was really tired and worn out from the pain and vomiting, so our family took me to the doctor. I couldn't stand or walk from the pain, so I crawled into the office on my hands and knees. The doctor checked me and said I had appendicitis. "You need to have emergency surgery right away." I told him, "I have stage 4 terminal cancer; I can't risk having surgery here. I need to go home and see my doctor. Give me a shot for pain, and I'll fly back home right now." He gave me a shot for the pain, and it worked right away. I was able to stand, so I told my wife, "Let's go home!" Our good friend Marcelo Fernandez picked us up and took us to the airport. We got on the first flight we could find and headed home. I was so worn out.

We arrived in Tijuana, crossed the border, picked up our car and drove all the way to Loma Linda hospital—about a two-hour drive. When we arrived, they took me into the emergency room and checked me to see where the pain was coming from. The pain was starting to come back while I was waiting. They finally got me into a room and put me on pain meds and decided I needed surgery right away.

The next morning, October 1, I had an emergency appendectomy. After the surgery, the doctor came in and said I was fortunate I had arrived there on time; my appendix was ready to rupture. It was so swollen it had to be pulled away from my skin. The next day, I left the hospital and went home with some discomfort from the surgery. What a relief.

A few months earlier, we were spending time with my family, and we shared about our trips to Mexico—about how fun it was, the food, the historical sites and so on. My sister Rachel said, "You guys need to go to Europe," so we began to plan it, and in October 2018, we were off on my first European vacation. My sister had been to Europe a few times, so she set everything up. She brought her husband, Ruben, two of her daughters and a couple of friends. My wife and my brother Edward were also on the trip. It was going to be great to spend time with my siblings.

It was going on eight months into my treatment, so my energy level was low from the infusions, and I would get fatigued easily. I wondered if it would be too much walking for me. Also, three weeks earlier, I had just had my appendectomy, so I took a wheelchair with me to help with all of the walking we would be doing. Thankfully there would be plenty of people to help push me along.

We flew out on October 25. Our first stop was London. We arrived at the airport and took the Tube from there to our rooms, then went to eat some fish and chips, a must-have in London. We took the Tube to our next stop, Buckingham Palace, but there was no sign of the Queen, unfortunately. The royal guards were cool to look at; they barely blink and don't move a muscle.

From there, we walked through St. James Park. We took some great pics there and headed to Carnaby Street in Soho. It's a cool, hip place. As we walked around, we saw a few famous theaters. We went to The Harry Potter Shop at Platform 9 ¾ and enjoyed our first day there in London.

My brother Ed and I are rock and rollers, so we wanted to check out some of the sites of famous rock stars. The next day, we went by the first place on our list, Freddie Mercury's house. From there, we went to a house Jimi Hendrix once lived in. We went to Abbey Road, and of course, all of us guys had to take a picture walking across the crosswalk, just like the Beatles did for their *Abbey Road* album cover.

That evening, my brother Ed, my wife and I went to a concert at the O2 arena to see Robert Plant and Van Morrison. What an experience to see Robert Plant live in London—one for the history books. We rocked out to all the hits he played. Led Zeppelin is our favorite rock band, so seeing Plant in London was a check on the bucket list, especially to have done it with my brother. It made the event much more special. It was also the fiftieth anniversary of when Led Zeppelin had formed: 1968 in London.

The next day, we rented cars for our day of excursions. It was pretty cool being able to drive a car with right-hand steering; a little awkward for shifting since I'm left-handed but I did it. It was an amazing experience driving through England on the opposite side of the road from where I normally drive in the United States, but you get used to it after a little while. Ed and I had planned to visit John Bonham's grave, the late drummer for Led

Zeppelin, but we got a late start in the morning, so we had to scratch it off the list.

Our first stop was Oxford University, the oldest university in the English-speaking world. The construction and facades are amazing. I took many pictures of the structures. Luckily for us, there was a J. R. R. Tolkien exhibit going on, so we attended the exhibit and were able to see many artifacts and browse through many of Tolkien's works.

From there, we went to The Eagle and Child pub, the place where the Inklings met up: famous writers like J. R. R. Tolkien, C. S. Lewis and other well-known authors would hang out there. We grabbed a bite to eat and then we were off to Stonehenge.

At Stonehenge, we walked through and marveled at the large stones. It was incredible to be at such a historic place. We took pictures and then went into the museum to learn more about Stonehenge's history. From there, we went back to our rooms in London and packed up to leave the next morning to our second stop: Paris.

The next day we landed in Paris, the City of Love. From the airport, we drove straight to the Eiffel Tower, and as we drove by, the sight was impressive. We took our pics and continued on our trip. We walked the streets and went by the Arc de Triomphe, and from there, we walked over to the Louvre museum. We had lunch and then went for a boat ride on the River Seine to see the sights from a river view.

The sun began to set as the boat made its way along the river. Lights came on all around, and the Eiffel Tower lit up. That was an amazing sight. We went to have dinner, and then went back to our rooms.

One of the places on our list of rock star sites was here in Paris: the grave of Jim Morrison, late singer of The Doors. Early in the morning the next day, we stopped at Père Lachaise

Cemetery to see Jim Morrison's grave. The cemetery is very Gothic. I took some great pictures there. My brother Ed and I walked through till we came to Jim's gravesite. It was awesome to visit the resting site of a great rock legend. We stood there in amazement and talked about our favorite hits, his movie and what it must have been like to see him live in concert. As we talked, we looked at all of the stuff placed around his grave: letters, drawings, gifts, pictures and so on. It was a somber moment. All I could think of was how this young talented guy from the United States wound up here. I had read about all of the details, but it was a sad story for me. We walked back to our car, where our family was patiently waiting and left.

From there we went to Giverny, the home and gardens of Claude Monet. The gardens are spectacular, with so many flowers, plants, trees and ponds. It's no wonder he would get inspired to paint there. On our way back we drove to the Palace of Versailles. Another beautiful place; so much to see in the palace and the amazing gardens outside.

From there, we separated from the group and had dinner with my sister Rachel and her husband Ruben. It was nice to sit and have a quiet dinner after all of the running around. After dinner, we met back up with the rest of our group and headed to the Eiffel Tower to get some night pics with the tower lit up. After that, we went back to our rooms, changed and went out to a local bar. That in itself was a cool experience. It seemed like everyone was staring at us. I'm sure they could tell we were tourists, but we had some drinks and had a great time.

The last evening of our trip, we set aside some time to get together and toast to our trip. We wanted to give thanks and express what we felt after traveling together. We had bought some wine, cheese and plenty of French goodies to munch on in preparation. My sister began saying she was grateful to have taken a trip with my brother Ed and me. "To be here with you guys is very special for me," she said. We had spent days together before on family trips, but to have been together so many days in Europe was unforgettable.

She mentioned that our dad must be smiling from up in Heaven seeing the three of us traveling together in Europe. She was grateful for the moments we spent together. She reminisced about how much we had laughed, talked and bonded throughout the whole trip. After she spoke, with tears in our eyes, the three of us embraced and gave each other a big hug. My wife's turn came, and she thanked God for giving us life and health to make this trip. She thanked Ruben and Rachel for inviting us and for making this such a great trip. She mentioned that we had wanted to come to Paris; we had tried to plan it on several occasions, but it had never came to fruition. This was God's plan and time for us to come. She knew bringing her to Paris was a lifelong dream of mine so that made being there really special. "I toast to my husband's health—cheers!"

My brother Ed began to share how special it was for him that the three of us got to see all of the sights together. He mentioned how great it was to see Robert Plant in London. Ed had just turned fifty, and the band Led Zeppelin was celebrating fifty years, and for us to celebrate that together was incredible. We were able to take some great pictures together. He was a little disappointed that he didn't get to see John Bonham's statue but wound up letting it go and focused on the trip; he remembered he wasn't traveling alone. It's hard for us sometimes to spend time together and put up with each other for so many days. Everyone laughed because Ed usually likes to pick on everyone and bug them, so we usually have to put up with him and his antics.

Then it was my turn. I thanked Ruben and Rachel also for helping us get on this trip to Europe; without their help it wouldn't have been possible. "When I was told eight months ago that I would live around a month, I thought life was over. To be here today, alive, in Europe with all of you, is a huge blessing. To have been able to walk around was awesome; I still have my challenges health-wise but to be able to eat and enjoy everything is truly a miracle; I am so blessed. I don't know what's coming. I have some tough challenges ahead—major surgery and who knows what else—but coming on this trip was a dream come true. Cheers!" As you can imagine, there wasn't a dry eye in the room. We couldn't have planned it any better. This was a trip for the history books.

FINAL THOUGHT

I would never have imagined this trip eight months before, but God had it planned out all along. This trip brought new life into me; I am inspired and full of joy. I was finally able to take my wife to Paris, checking one more thing off my bucket list. To have done this trip with my brother and my sister was the icing on the cake; what a blessing.

I'm glad I made the sacrifice to go on this trip. There were times before and during the trip when I thought I might get sick or not have the strength to do so much. Physically, it was very challenging but in the end, it was well worth it. I would definitely do it all over again. Thank you, God, for my family and for this wonderful trip.

FILLING OURSELVES WITH THE LOVE OF GOD

EPHESIANS 3:17–19

Then Christ will make his home in your hearts as you trust in him. Your roots will grow down into God's love and keep you strong. And may you have the power to understand, as all God's people should, how wide, how long, how high, and how deep his love is. May you experience the love of Christ, though it is too great to understand fully. Then you will be made complete with all the fullness of life and power that comes from God.

Chapter Eighteen

EMBRACE THE TICKING CLOCK

Ruben, enjoying life! Freedom.

JAMES 4:14 NIV
*Why, you do not even know what will happen
tomorrow. What is your life? You are a mist that
appears for a little while and then vanishes.*

JOB 7:7 NIV
*Remember, O God, that my life is but a breath;
my eyes will never see happiness again.*

Life is short. Live it up! Be happy! (No matter what your circumstances are.) We always tend to take life for granted. To live is incredible! Every morning when I open my eyes, I am amazed! WOW! I'm alive! ANOTHER DAY! I can see, I can walk, my arms move!

After my surgery, I had to depend on others to bring me food and drinks, to bathe me, to help me get up, to dress me. It is something I never want to experience again. I never want to take for granted all that I have. No matter what the circumstances are, even with stage 4 terminal cancer, I am alive today! I'm blessed. I need to make the best of today. Whether I'm alone or in the company of my family or friends, I will enjoy today. No one, I repeat, no one is guaranteed tomorrow.

If you've been wanting to go somewhere or do something, do it! If you're craving something, get it! Make it! Skydive, take a trip, make that phone call—you're alive, you're free, be radical!

There is no time for worry, stress, fear or anxiety.

I see couples not submitting to one another. Waiting to resolve issues in their marriage. "I'm not ready!" one says. "We need to get some counseling first"—excuse after excuse. Family members are divided. I'll talk to them and they say, "When I or they get over it." What if I told you today will be the last day that you'll be alive? Or that today is the last day for your spouse, your parents, your neighbor, your old friend or your family member? You're going to wake up tomorrow and receive a call that one of those people is gone. It happens, just like that. We think we have time … how wrong we are.

"This is what I have observed to be good: that it is appropriate for a person to eat, to drink and to find satisfaction in their toilsome labor under the sun during **the few days of life God has given them**—for this is their lot.

"Moreover, when God gives someone wealth and possessions, and the ability to enjoy them, to accept their lot and be happy in their toil—this is a gift of God. They seldom reflect on the days of their life, because God keeps them occupied with gladness of heart." (Ecclesiastes 5:18-20 NIV)

"For the despondent, every day brings trouble; for the happy heart, life is a continual feast." (Proverbs 15:15 NLT)

Dictionary definitions of "despondent," by the way, include 1) Feeling or showing extreme discouragement, dejection, or depression; 2) In low spirits from loss of hope or courage; and 3) Feeling or showing profound hopelessness, dejection, discouragement, or gloom.

Once you die, there are no more chances to be happy here on Earth or to make things right.

God has given you today. Be happy and make the best of it. What will you do with your today and the opportunities it brings?

Who are you going to call? Or visit?

Do you know how many people say, "If I just had one more chance to make it right, I'd take it"? For many, it's too late. For you, you have today. I ask again, what will you do with your today? LET GO!!! And LET'S GO!!! Get on with your today! Happy life, today!

Life is short.

My friend Matty McLain once said, "Sometimes when people ask what it's like living with metastatic cancer, I tell them to imagine walking around with a backpack on and inside that backpack is a bomb. You have no idea when that bomb is going to go off; it could go off today or tomorrow, a year from now or ten years from now ... it might never go off (although that seems unlikely, because you can hear it ticking).

"You can hear it ticking, tick, tick, tick, knowing that at any moment this bomb can go off and blow your life up. You try to get by, making plans for the future and whatnot but always in the back of your mind wondering if your bomb will go off before then."

Although this is something people like myself live with when you have stage 4 terminal cancer, isn't it also true for everyone? No one knows when they're going to die.

I once asked the question to an audience, "When are you going to die?" There was no response. I didn't even hear the crickets make a noise. Most people were in shock at the question and just looked at me with a blank stare, some with watery eyes.

I've realized you don't have to have stage 4 terminal cancer to die. You can have an accident at any given moment; you can get sick with many and any type of illness and die. While on this cancer journey, I've seen several family members, friends and–as I read the news daily–so many famous people pass away. A lot of those people were perfectly healthy.

It almost sounds clichéd to tell you, "Tell those close to you that you love them every moment you can"; tomorrow is not promised to anyone."

FINAL THOUGHT

I talk to people all of the time, and everyone is always going through something, so they think. We usually make things out to be bigger than they actually are and let it ruin our attitude, and especially our day. The bad part is everyone around us gets reeled into our problems and our bad attitude.

You've heard the saying, "If Momma ain't happy, nobody's happy!" Well, sometimes it's Daddy, or a child, or your friend or whoever you may be around who's miserable for no apparent reason. It all starts with the opening of your eyes when you wake up in the morning. We must begin with an attitude of gratitude. Keep in mind that you may not have this opportunity tomorrow. Be happy today, no matter what situation you may awaken to; make the best of the day God has blessed you with.

Chapter Nineteen

LET THE LITTLE CHILDREN COME TO ME

Ruby Nevaeh Narváez (my granddaughter) during
our last trip together for Memorial Day in 2021.

REVELATION 21:4,7
*He will wipe every tear from their eyes, and there
will be no more death or sorrow or crying or pain.
All these things are gone forever ... All who are
victorious will inherit all these blessings, and I will
be their God, and they will be my children.*

On September 29, 2021, I was on a trip to Europe. I had gone on a trip with my wife, my mother-in-law, my sister Rachel, her family and friends, and my brother Danny and his family. We were stopping in Paris for a day, and it would be my first time touring Italy.

My wife, my mother-in-law and I spent that first day in Paris touring the Eiffel Tower during the day and then went back in the evening to see the tower lit up. After a long day, we finally got to our room around midnight. Thirty minutes later, I got a call from my son Chris. He sounded emotional and desperate, and was crying. He said, "Dad, I just got a call that Ruby died. Can you please go down there and check on her? Hurry, Dad! Please!

I said, "Son, we're in Paris; we just arrived today. Let me call Gabriel and Gaby so they can go down there and confirm that it's true. I called them and had them rush down to Ruby's grandma's house. I told them, "Call me as soon as you find out!"

A few minutes later, Gaby called me and crying uncontrollably said, "Dad, it's true Ruby has passed away! She's lying in the driveway covered in a blanket that's full of blood." At that moment I began to cry uncontrollably. No! No! No! It couldn't be true! I confirmed the news to my wife and my mother-in-law and the three of us wept together.

As we wept for hours, I realized that we had to go home, now! I called the airline to try and catch the soonest flight out. After long wait times and trying for hours, I wasn't able to get a response. I was in such desperation and was drained emotionally. I said to my wife, "We need to relax. We need some inspiration; let's go to God."

We prayed and gave God all of our worries. We prayed for our son, for all of our kids and family, and we also prayed for all of those close to Ruby—her mom, her grandparents and so on. We knew they were hurting as much as we were.

I prayed for God to comfort us with Scriptures, so I began to read. I came along Revelations 21. In verses 3-4 it says, "I heard a loud shout from the throne, saying, 'Look, God's home is now among his people! He will live with them, and they will be his people. God himself will be with them. ⁴He will wipe every tear from their eyes, and there will be no more death or sorrow or crying or pain. All these things are gone forever.'"

I said to my wife, "Ruby is in Heaven now—no more tears, no more death, sorrow or pain." As I kept reading, in verse 7 it says, "All who are victorious will inherit all these blessings, and I will be their God, and they will be my children." In verse 8 it goes on to talk about sinners; their fate is the fiery lake of burning sulfur—Hell. I continued telling my wife, "Ruby was only eleven. She hadn't sinned yet; she was innocent, she was victorious!" I said, "Ruby is resting in paradise; she's in peace."

Those thoughts comforted me so much, knowing she was with God and no longer suffering here on earth. Was I still hurting? Of course I was; the pain was unbearable. Ruby was our oldest granddaughter; we had spent the most time with her. We had her for sleepovers, and she had tagged along with us on every trip to the river, vacations or just a quick trip to downtown LA.

Through these Scriptures I found peace. They brought much-needed comfort. Thank God for His Scriptures and for my faith. I had talked to Ruby about lying before because she had once tried to stretch the truth about a situation so I made it clear that lying is wrong, that lies are awful and how lies hurt people. She really took it to heart and changed her behavior.

Every time she'd come over to visit, she would spill the beans about everything, opening up to the truth of things that happened. She was very honest and had a big heart. I am completely convinced she is in Heaven now.

We had barely had any sleep and our flight to Italy was in the morning, so we hurried out and headed to the airport, caught our flight and landed in Italy. We got to our hotel, settled in and got to work on getting a flight back. The airline we flew on had filed for bankruptcy just before we left, and the state had taken it over so getting through and getting information over the phone was impossible.

The next day my sister Rachel and I went down to the airport in person, and I was able to get to a counter to get our flights changed. I explained the situation and the lady said that with all the changes the airline was going through, the soonest flight would be on Monday (three days later), so I took it and headed back to our hotel.

I talked it over with my wife and told her, "We don't leave for three days. There's nothing we can change with Ruby's passing. I definitely want to get back to our kids as soon as possible so we can be together as they are all in mourning. Tomorrow is your mom's eighty-first birthday; let's make the best of these three days and enjoy them with her."

We spent the day in Rome visiting the tourist sites, ate some great food, and of course we had to get some gelato. We went to Florence the next day, and the following day we went to Venice for a quick gondola ride, took the train back to Rome and flew back home.

We finally made it back home to our kids. We walked into our home and as soon as we saw each other, all our emotions overwhelmed us. We had a good cry and gave many hugs to each other; we were finally together. They filled us in on what had happened and what the future plans were so far with Ruby's funeral preparations.

Due to the COVID situation, it took about six weeks to finally get Ruby's body back to do her service and funeral. We had her service on November 5, 2021. The night of her service, I gave her eulogy and shared a message. I told everyone about receiving the news while in Paris and I shared the Scriptures in Revelations 21. I shared a few other Scriptures and reminded them of how short life really is. I mentioned that maybe someone sitting in the audience may not make it to the funeral the next day; accidents happen, and you may be in a life-changing accident on the way out tonight or on the way to the funeral; you never know.

I asked, "What message is God trying to tell us as we see an eleven-year-old girl in a casket?" The message is, life is short. We never know when our last day is or at what moment death will find us. We were on vacation; you never know where you'll be when your life ends.

We had Ruby's funeral the next day, and I can honestly say it was the most difficult thing I've ever done in my life. Saying goodbye and seeing the casket being lowered into the ground was the most soul-crushing, painful event I've had to experience. There were so many emotions.

Little did I know this wouldn't be the only funeral we would be having before the end of the year.

FINAL THOUGHT

Nothing in this life is as painful as losing a child; the pain is inexplicable. I had many plans for Ruby, for her future. I am grateful that I was able to spend a lot of quality time with her. She always expressed her feelings, her thoughts and her emotions.

I miss her so much. She loved me unconditionally; she was so expressive. She was such a great helper and companion. She wasn't just my granddaughter, she was one of my best friends; she was my little angel.

Chapter Twenty

OUR TIME OF GRIEF

Maria Elena Garcia (my mom).

A TIME FOR EVERYTHING

E C C L E S I A S T E S 3 : 1 - 4
For everything there is a season, a time for every activity under heaven. A time to be born and a time to die. A time to plant and a time to harvest. A time to kill and a time to heal. A time to tear down and a time to build up. A time to cry and a time to laugh. A time to grieve and a time to dance.

A few weeks after Ruby's funeral, my mom got COVID and wound up in the hospital. After a week in the hospital, her COVID was gone but she still had pneumonia to deal with. The hospital tried to send her home with oxygen tanks once the COVID was gone but my mom resisted. She wanted to be free of any dangers from the pneumonia.

Monday went by, Tuesday passed and on Wednesday she began to feel a pain in her lung. Several of my siblings and I spoke to her throughout the day, and she was complaining about the pain getting stronger and more difficult to deal with.

As the evening came, her pain was unbearable. She insisted on getting pain meds to control it, but her pain wasn't managed well and the trauma took away all of her strength.

I woke up at 2:30 a.m. that Thursday morning, December 9, and as I was watching the news on my phone, it rang. It was my mom. I answered and said, "Hi Mom, how are you feeling?"

She said, "I'm dying; I can't breathe."

I screamed "Mom, Mom! What's going on?" Then the phone was hung up.

I immediately called the hospital and asked to be transferred to the department where my mom was. The nurse answered and I asked, "Is this where Maria Garcia is?"

She responded, "You know this is where she's at; you've called before!" I explained to her that I had never called before and that my sisters Rachel and Ana had been in charge of contacting the doctor and nurses to communicate the information to us—all eight siblings.

The nurse said "Okay, let me check to see what's going on." She came back on the phone and said my mom was being attended to by a nurse. They had given her Ativan and that my mom was hyperventilating. She assured me that she would be fine, that the doctor had been in at 2:30 a.m. and said all of her vitals were fine and that she was doing well.

I spoke to my sister Rachel after I hung up and filled her in. At 4:30 a.m., Rachel got a call from the doctor saying Mom wasn't doing well and that they were going to put her in the ICU.

Rachel asked the doctor, "How did my mom go from being fine at 2:30 a.m. when you checked on her to going into ICU now two hours later?" The doctor explained it was necessary and that her health was deteriorating. At 5:30 a.m. the doctor called Rachel again and said Mom had worsened and that they needed to intubate her.

"My mom didn't want to be intubated," Rachel told the doctor.

He said, "Well, if we don't intubate her, she's going to die."

So, we made the decision to intubate her. As soon as they intubated her, she had a stroke. The staff was able to get her stable only to have Mom have a second stroke. The doctor communicated that they were going to keep her in observation. Around 4:00 p.m. the doctor called and said Mom's kidneys had stopped functioning and that she may get sepsis. The doctor recommended doing dialysis, but at this point she was too weak.

They gave her some meds to help strengthen her and hopefully enable them to do the procedure. They prepared her and waited. At 7:30 p.m., she had another stroke. At that point the doctor said, "She's had three strokes. I recommend that if she has another one, you guys should let her go. Her eyes aren't reacting to the light anymore. Talk it over with your family and let me know."

We were all together at Ana's house and decided it would be best to not revive her if she had another stroke. At 10:30 p.m. that night she had another stroke. They kept her on a ventilator while we rushed down to the hospital so we could all see her one last time alive.

Because of COVID, no one had been allowed to enter until we had come to this point. They took her off the ventilator, and in pairs we began to go in to see her. The first two pairs of my siblings got to see her still breathing, but by the time the rest of us went in, she had passed.

Another tragedy to end the year. Life is short.

My mom had been perfectly healthy. I had tried to spend as much time as I could with her because of my terminal illness, which wound up being a blessing for me: the many times we had had breakfast together alone and with my siblings, and my nieces and nephews, and the amazing nine days we had spent touring through Mexico together, getting her to finally eat mole poblano in Puebla.

The many conversations we had had over the phone and in person. The many drives we had gone on to LA and several other cities. We were able to make some great memories and spend lots of quality time together. I'm glad she was almost always open to do stuff in an instant. I would call and ask her, "What are you up to?"

She'd say, "I just have to go to Ross and exchange some stuff but I can do that another day."

"Okay, great; you want to go with me to _____?"

"Sure, let's go!"

She knew my days were numbered, and as I was her eldest, I know she constantly wanted time together. I also know she worried about my health but my mom also knew about my faith in God. She had gone to many church services with my wife and me. She'd always remind me, "Man, God really loves you, son." I miss my mom dearly and will treasure our memories together.

I felt pain with her passing, but after losing Ruby I was out of tears and my emotions were still so numb. There are moments of shock when I remember that she's gone; I still can't believe it. I've lost friends and have seen other people pass away, all reminders of how short life is. But losing a loved one, a parent, spouse, especially a child—I've realized there's nothing harder than losing a child.

No one can imagine the pain. I hope you never have to experience it. It goes against the grain of nature that God created. A child is supposed to bury their parents; a parent should never have to bury their child. Now GO! Tell your loved ones how much you love them; hug them tight, kiss them, forgive them.

If they don't live close by, at least give them a call and express your most intimate feelings. If they live far, be radical; find the next flight out, or if that's not possible, then plan a trip out there, soon!

If you can drive there, GO! Enjoy the scenery and little towns on your way. Take a bus, a train, whatever you need to do—do it! Don't let today pass without making the effort; tomorrow is not guaranteed to anyone, not even you. You can't imagine the joy you'll receive from those memories you'll create by stepping out of your comfort zone or by simply putting in a little effort; it's a win-win for everyone involved.

Traveling has been an incredible experience for me and for those who have come along for the ride. As of this writing, I have traveled to Europe a third time and have traveled through twenty-one of the thirty-one states in Mexico. There's so much to see that I've traveled to some states multiple times; I'm a pro now. There are ten states left for me to explore. If God is willing and my health permits, my goal is to travel to those last ten states. What a great bucket list item to check off. All of this traveling, thanks to me getting cancer. Don't wait for something tragic to happen in your life. Go and travel; you will thank me later.

God bless you, and may He bless every moment you spend with the people you love. Above all, enjoy the adventure of every day.

FINAL THOUGHT

My emotions are in shambles. Two people who were so close to me are now gone, just like that. The holidays won't be the same without them. I'm not sure what things will happen in the future but for now I will continue to enjoy every day God gives me and make the best of every moment I get to spend with my loved ones. Never has life seemed so meaningless and so meaningful.

Chapter Twenty-One

THE GOD OF ALL COMFORT

Aztec souvenir, depicting the three phases
of life: birth, life, and death.

ROMANS 8:35, 37-39

*Can anything ever separate us from Christ's love?
Does it mean he no longer loves us if we have trouble or
calamity, or are persecuted, or hungry, or destitute, or in
danger, or threatened with death? ...
No, despite all these things, overwhelming victory is ours
through Christ, who loved us. And I am convinced that
nothing can ever separate us from God's love. Neither*

death nor life, neither angels nor demons, neither our fears
for today nor our worries about tomorrow—not even the
powers of hell can separate us from God's love. No power
in the sky above or in the earth below—indeed, nothing
in all creation will ever be able to separate us from the
love of God that is revealed in Christ Jesus our Lord.

That's amazing! This is a powerful Scripture. NOTHING can separate us from the love of God. I don't know about you, but I am convinced. I am grateful and I feel really loved by God; I am blessed.

The reality is that after losing my mom and Ruby, death is more present than ever. How much time do I have left? The clock is constantly ticking and so are my thoughts; their deaths are reminders of how fragile life is, whether you're ill or perfectly healthy.

My mom was seventy-three years old, had eight kids, twenty-seven grandchildren and twelve great-grandchildren. She was blessed with a large family; for me that is so fulfilling. To have left her mark through her family is remarkable; not many people leave such an impact. If you look at every one of the forty-seven family members, we all have a characteristic of my mom, especially her eight children. There are so many pictures, memories of the days when she was young in Mexico and pics of when she had just arrived in the United States. She always told us stories of when she arrived and began junior high at Hollenbeck in East LA. There are pics of when she began her life with my dad, when I was born—the story goes on and on.

Those memories give me much satisfaction and fill my heart with peace. Do I miss her? Yes, of course. She wasn't done yet, but there was a lot she was able to do and accomplish.

On the other hand, with Ruby passing away at eleven years old–that's so painful and difficult to come to peace with. I have pictures of her in her mommy's tummy and pics of her from day one when she was born to the day she passed. I will never have pictures of her in high school, her quinceañera, her graduation, her wedding or of her children. Those memories will never come to fruition; she's gone. Life was short for her. In the eleven years she lived, she left a great impact in many people's lives. She genuinely loved you–that was her staple. She really cared for everyone, young and old. She always gave special attention to the younger kids and that always made me feel like she was going to be a great mother. If people came over with kids, they never had to worry about their kids; Ruby would always take charge and the kids would love hanging out with her. She would bring out crafts or games and entertain them.

To the adults, she was always helpful. "Would you like something to drink? Can I get you anything?" She would chat about everything; she could carry a conversation with anyone. Everyone who met Ruby was impacted; they never forgot her. Her funeral service was packed with family, friends, teachers and neighbors. Everyone had a story of how special Ruby was. I can only wonder about the great things she was going to do and what an amazing family she would have had.

I remember when my dad passed away at sixty-seven; I thought he was too young to go. Then when I was diagnosed with cancer and was given a short time to live at fifty-two, I was really not ready to go. At that point in my life, my wife and I were about to take the next step in our marriage. Celebrating twenty-five years of marriage, traveling together, making great memories together, doing things we had never done before, now that we had the liberty of not having small children to care for. My kids, although they're adults, still need me. I want to enjoy my grandchildren more and watch them grow up. I want to see my great-grandchildren someday. Now I wonder if any of these things will be possible. Only God knows. The doctors don't have a positive outlook, but I do. I am going against the grain, but I am going to enjoy every day I am given. I will be joyful every day, no matter what comes, and I will be on an adventure every day even when I am sitting in my chair getting another infusion.

My last day will be when God opens the door to Heaven for me. For now, I will take everything in stride. I have plans, short term and long. While I am physically able, I will run, I will walk, I will climb and I will fly to wherever my heart desires. No holding back, no excuses, no compromises. What cancer? God loves me! Nothing can separate me from His love. I'm off to where the sun rises and to where the sun sets. Who wants to come along?

FINAL THOUGHT

I have a souvenir I bought in Mexico. It's an Aztec piece that depicts the three parts of our lives: birth, life and death. We all go through the three phases. Death is coming to all of us. The mystery is, we never know when it will happen or in which way.

Live as if today is your last day or a loved one's last day. God loves each and every one of us profoundly, so let God's love comfort you and take away anything that hinders you from enjoying your life. God bless.

The Final Recipe

Thank you for taking the time to read my story. I'm glad you made it through and hope you feel like you've walked alongside with me. I hope you are inspired, encouraged and ready for any challenge you may face in your life. May God bless you in your walk and through those moments when you need Him most. I wish you the best on your journey.

Over the course of my book, I shared 5 ingredients:

1. Fear of God

2. Being Joyful in Hope

3. Being Patient in Affliction

4. Being Faithful in Prayer

5. Filling Ourselves with the Love of God

1ST INGREDIENT: FEAR OF GOD

PROVERBS 1:7
*The fear of the Lord is the beginning of knowledge,
but fools despise wisdom and instruction.*

The Scripture says it all: to begin to have knowledge, we must fear God.

PSALMS 112:1
Praise the Lord! How joyful are those who fear the Lord and delight in obeying his commands.

PSALMS 112:6-7
Such people will not be overcome by evil. Those who are righteous will be long remembered. ⁷They do not fear bad news; they confidently trust the Lord to care for them.

First ingredient: Fear of God.

There are two types of fear, servile fear and filial fear.

Servile fear suggests the behavior of one in forced servitude, such as a servant or a slave. In other words, I obey God (my boss, my master) because I am afraid he will punish me if I am disobedient. That type of fear (servile) distances me from God, this is not a close relationship.

Filial fear is the fear a son or daughter may have towards their parents. The Mirriam-webster definition for filial (adjective) of, relating to a son or daughter Filial Has Familial Origins. Filial comes from Latin filius, meaning "son," and filia, "daughter"; in English, it applies to both genders. The word has long carried the dutiful sense "owed to a parent by a child," as found in such phrases as "filial respect" and "filial piety." These days it can also be used more generally for any emotion or behavior of a child to a parent.

When we have filial fear we obey God because we don't want to hurt our relationship. I don't want to do anything that might demonstrate that I don't love Him or respect Him. "I'll obey you God because I love you" especially because you love me so much. It draws me towards God.

We need to have filial fear towards God. To have filial fear of God means that we have awe and respect toward the majesty of God. We recognize who He is.

Fear of the Lord brings joy. Those who fear God are always happy, no matter the circumstances. They also delight in obeying His commands. That type of fear brings reverence and trust in the almighty. I'm not afraid of God. He loves me and would never harm me. Fear of Him gives me joy, knowing how powerful He is. He can protect me at all times from anything, even from cancer. He's kept me alive this far, even after the doctors said to get my affairs in order and prepare for my funeral almost five years ago.

Verses 6–7 in Psalms 112 say, "They (those who fear God) do not fear bad news; they confidently trust the Lord to care for them." I received the worst news of my life when my granddaughter Ruby passed away. Hearing I had stage 4 cancer and that I was going to die was bad, but the news of Ruby passing away was worse news by far.

The day I was told I would die soon wasn't welcome news, but that day I was still alive. I had to be happy for that day, at least. When you hear of a death, it's over; there's no coming back from that.

What would be the worst news for you? That you lost your job? You've been robbed? Your car was stolen? You lost your home? You have a terminal illness? You're going to die? Your child or your spouse has passed away?

Imagine not fearing any of those things. God wants us to have that trust in Him, that type of security. That whatever happens in our lives, we will continue to trust Him and continue to be joyful.

That's not an easy task, but it is achievable when you have fear of the Lord.

Ecclesiastes 12:13 tells us, "That's the whole story. Here now is my final conclusion: Fear God and obey his commands, for this is everyone's duty."

As Christians, Fear of God is our duty, and to obey His commands. Remember Psalms 112? "How joyful are those who fear the Lord and delight in obeying His commands."

Do you want to be happy in all circumstances? First ingredient, fear God.

2ND INGREDIENT: BEING JOYFUL IN HOPE

Romans 12:12
Be joyful in hope, patient in affliction, faithful in prayer.

This Scripture contains Ingredients 2-4, the second of which is to be joyful in hope. NLT says "Rejoice in our hope"; YOU have to be joyful. First of all, what is your hope? It is something to really consider. We all should have hope, and we should rejoice in our hope.

I am not going to delve too much into hope. Hope is going to be an ingredient you put in; after all, it is going to be a part of your own recipe. Without hope, we are lost; there is no future, and we are just wandering through life without a purpose.

I would encourage you to go to your Bible concordance and look up the word *hope*. Read at least ten Scriptures, but if you're really eager to find hope, read twenty-five Scriptures or more. You will get a good perspective on what hope is and what to hope for so you can rejoice in your hope.

JOB 11:18
Having hope will give you courage. You will be protected and will rest in safety.

Hope will give you courage for when you are confronted with challenges in life. The Scripture also says, "You will be protected," so hope helps us with our insecurities. The Scripture says, "You will rest in safety"; another version says, "You will sleep confidently."

Do you have sleepless or restless nights? Hope will give you the peace you need to rest and sleep comfortably without worry.

3RD INGREDIENT: BEING PATIENT IN AFFLICTION

YOU have to be patient in affliction. This is a difficult one because most of us find it hard to be patient when there is no affliction, so patience in affliction will be one we have to work on and may take some time to learn and put into practice.

At this moment, although this is a difficult time in my life, I feel I am not in affliction. Although recently, I have to confess, I was feeling tired of having cancer, tired of the infusions, and sometimes my emotions get the better of me. I repented and prayed to be grateful for another day of life.

For physical pain I would have to refer to post-surgery. That was the most physical pain I have ever felt in my life. I was given plenty of medication to help with the pain, and although I didn't want the medication, I didn't have a choice if I wanted to recover. After I was awakened from a coma and in my hospital room, the nurses would come in to give me another pill or give me another injection for pain. Every time they came in, I had to fight the anxiety in my mind.

I didn't want pain medication; I was completely against it. I had to trust that it was for my own good—that I needed to be patient and let the doctors do their job. As the days passed, it became part of my daily routine. Several times a day, I was given pain medication. Eventually I went home and thought, *I'm done with those pain medications*. But once the pain started, it didn't take long for me to realize I still needed them. After a few days, I was able to wean myself off them and be comfortable.

That is how I learned to be patient in physical affliction.

For emotional affliction, the most emotional pain I have ever felt was when I lost my granddaughter Ruby. I had so many thoughts running through my mind, especially all the what-ifs.

My dad once told me, "Let the emotional pain go through your heart, not through your mind. Keep it here," (pointing to his heart) "don't let it get up here" (pointing to his temple). He was right. If you think about it in your mind, you'll go crazy—lose total control—whereas if you let it go through your heart, you'll deal with it in a different way. You'll cry—and depending on the affliction, probably cry uncontrollably—but you will avoid the anger and frustration that your mind will produce.

In our minds, especially when going through an affliction, we lose our patience right away; afflictions affect our reasoning. If we are patient in affliction, things will always be resolved and dealt with in a calm manner without causing pain to others, especially to ourselves.

4TH INGREDIENT: BEING FAITHFUL IN PRAYER

YOU MUST be faithful in prayer. Sometimes when we are in affliction, we're angry or hurt, so the last thing we want to do is pray. No matter what the affliction is, we need to pray all the way through it, constantly.

Honestly, I can say that prayer is the only thing that has brought me peace in my most difficult afflictions. When I cast my afflictions and cares upon God through prayer, I am releasing them from my mind; I am laying the burden on God. Those requests I pass on to Him are things I have no control of and can no longer handle emotionally. The pain is still in my heart—that takes time to heal—but the burden of my afflictions is God's.

In the last four years, I have received so much unwanted news. When I was first told I was going to die and had a short time to live, I cried out in prayer to God. "Did you hear what the doctor said?! What are you going to do with that?" I was somewhat upset with the news, but I knew there was nothing I could do but pray and give it to God. He is the Almighty.

When the pandemic started, they stopped allowing visitors into the hospital, so I started going to my appointments by myself. One day I went in for a CT scan and the results showed that the cancer had spread to several organs. Being that I was alone, the news was difficult to swallow. Walking out, my emotions were running high; honestly, I was worried. My eyes were tearing up and at that moment I knew I had to pray. I couldn't carry that burden either. It was too much.

It took a few days of prayer to finally regain my composure and realize that I was still alive and trusting that God was in control of the situation. Later in the year, I went in for another appointment and the oncologist said these could be the last six months of my life. This time as the news came, I directly gave it to God in prayer.

It isn't always that easy, but practice makes perfect. I still don't have it completely under control because I am an emotional man. I always try to prepare myself for anything, but you can always get caught off guard. Luckily God is always there to listen.

Stay faithful in prayer.

5TH INGREDIENT: FILLING YOURSELF WITH THE LOVE OF GOD

EPHESIANS 3:17–19

Then Christ will make his home in your hearts as you trust in him. Your roots will grow down into God's love and keep you strong. [18]And may you have the power to understand, as all God's people should, how wide, how long, how high, and how deep his love is. [19]May you experience the love of Christ, though it is too great to understand fully. Then you will be made complete with all the fullness of life and power that comes from God.

Verse 17 says, "Your roots will grow down into God's love and keep you strong."

Only having deep roots into God's love will keep you strong. If we don't have deep roots, we'll be weak.

Verse 18 says, "And may you have the power to understand." Maybe you don't understand how wide, how long, how high and how deep God's love is for you.

Verse 19 says, "May you experience the love of Christ … Then, you will be made complete."

The fifth ingredient is to fill yourself with the love of God. Most people have never experienced the full love of God, so they are incomplete. Life seems unfair. Why me? We are never pleased; always empty, and we have uncontrolled emotions.

If we don't understand or have the fullness of God's love, life is miserable. Nothing else will ever satisfy us like God's love. You know the saying, "Sticks and stones may break my bones, but words can never hurt me?" Well I say, "Death and pain may come, but the love of God will always protect me."

We need to fill up on God's love. God has a lot of love for us; it's unlimited, even more when we're going through troublesome times. I constantly feel so loved by God. I feel spoiled rotten at times.

He shows me so much love and affection, and I love it, I take it all in. I'm fully at peace; nothing bothers me when I let God love me with everything He's got. At times when I sin or don't behave as I should, I can feel like I'm not deserving of so much love. I have to remind myself that I am forgiven, that God is my Father, that I am His child, that He loves me with all of His heart and that He forgives my sins.

The devil always tries to convince us that we're not deserving of God's love or deserving of His forgiveness, but God's love overpowers those thoughts. We try to fill ourselves with the things we love: our children, our spouses, work, sports, hobbies and sometimes even with church duties, and those things don't fill us or satisfy us like we want them to.

When it comes to receiving God's love, we don't know what to do with it. We aren't sure how to receive it because we haven't experienced so much love. The only love we have known is conditional. God is trying to love us unconditionally and most of the time we push that love away.

Let's let Him love us with everything. Let's open our hearts and take it all in.

There you have it—the secret recipe to happiness, no matter what happens in life. To God be the glory!

My future plans are to seek opportunities to speak at congregations and events where I can encourage and inspire others with my testimony and experience.

I am also venturing into becoming a grief recovery counselor to help others with their emotional healing and any needs they may have from challenges and difficult times in their lives.

I will be planning and taking groups of people on trips. If you and your friends or family would like to go on a tour or vacation, get on board!

I look forward to sharing news with you of upcoming opportunities for book signings and events, and future trips that I will be attending and promoting. Please sign up at www.faithpositivitytravel.com to stay updated on the latest information.

Thank you to all my family and friends whom I mentioned in the book and for those whom I didn't mention (you know who you are) who have prayed, encouraged and been by my side through my journey.

A special thanks to one of my best friends, Marcelo Fernandez. On one of our several trips together, I mentioned I would like to write a book, and he said DO IT! He convinced me. He said my children, grandchildren, great grandchildren and generations to come could read my book and would benefit from it. He told me that I would leave it as a legacy for my family.

And thank you again for taking the time to read my story. May God bless you in your walk. I wish you the best on your journey.

Ruben Narváez Garcia